D0002963

Hello, Stranger WITHDRAWN

"...insights from a time when a young person with autism grew up in a world where nobody understood them!"
—Temple Grandin, author of *Thinking in Pictures*

"An extraordinary look at autism from the inside—by turns heartbreaking, uplifting, illuminating, witty, and wise."
—Steve Silberman, author of *NeuroTribes: The Legacy of Autism and the Future of Neurodiversity*

"Remarkably detailed, stunningly honest, and, in the end, deeply moving. A unique look into the heart and mind of someone who never fit in."
—Rachel Simon, author of *Riding the Bus with My Sister*

"A testament to neurodiversity and a call to acceptance."
—Martha Leary, author of *Autism: Sensory-Movement Differences and Diversity*

"This book is a winner for all to read. It clearly reveals the contrast between the world view and experiences of one remarkable person with autism and those around her ..."
—Nancy Minshew, MD, founder, Center for Excellence in Autism Research at the University of Pittsburgh

"An uncommon soul navigating the pain and triumph of self-discovery."
—William Stillman, award-winning author of *The Soul of Autism* and *Empowered Autism Parenting*

"As sweet and honest and painful and true and illuminating as any personal story you will ever read."
—Paula Kluth, Ph.D., author of *You're Going to Love This Kid: Teaching Students with Autism in the Inclusive Classroom*

Hello, Stranger

MY LIFE ON THE AUTISM SPECTRUM

Barbara Moran

• • • as told to Karl Williams

LIBRARY OF CONGRESS CATALOGING-IN-PUBLICATION DATA
Names: Moran, Barbara, 1951 May 29- author.
Title: Hello, stranger / by Barbara Moran ; as told to Karl Williams.
Description: Georgetown, Ohio : KiCam Projects, [2018].
Identifiers: LCCN 2018057782 (print) | LCCN 2018059924 (ebook) | ISBN 9780999742266 (ebook) | ISBN 9780999742259 (paperback) | ISBN 9780999742266
(ebook)
Subjects: LCSH: Moran, Barbara, 1951 May 29---Health. | Autistic people--United States--Biography. | Autism spectrum disorders.
Classification: LCC RC553.A88 (ebook) | LCC RC553.A88 M668 2018 (print) | DDC
616.85/882--dc23
LC record available at https://lccn.loc.gov/2018057782

Cover and book design by Mark Sullivan

ISBN 978-0-9997422-5-9 (paperback)
ISBN 978-0-9997422-6-6 (e-book)

Printed in the United States of America

Published by KiCam Projects

www.KiCamProjects.com

TABLE OF CONTENTS

INTRODUCTION
By Karl Williams

You won't find much in this book on theories about or treatment for autism. In a sense, this work is the byproduct of a friendship. I met Barbara Moran when my wife invited Barb and her sister, Ruth, to tell Barb's story at a conference in Hershey, Pennsylvania.

Born in 1951, Barb had clearly been very bright, but once she started school, her teachers might have used the word "undisciplined" to describe her. The term "autism" had only recently begun to appear in medical journals in the early Fifties[1], and beyond blaming the parents (the phrase "refrigerator mother" dates from this period), there were few theories—and no help. And so Barb ended up trapped in the mental health system for decades, misdiagnosed, until Ruth became a doctor.

I was fascinated. And there was no separating Barb's story from Barb herself—quite a character with her outlandish clothing choices, her outspoken ways, and her colorful drawings of traffic signals and cathedrals with spindly arms and legs and open-book faces.

Over lunch, following the conference in Hershey, we talked about working on a book together.

I've written two as-told-to autobiographies with leaders in the self-advocacy movement (people with intellectual disabilities working for respect and civil rights). Using transcriptions of recorded conversations, I removed all my questions and comments and worked exclusively with the words of those two remarkable men in order to render their stories in print.

---

1. "Autism" was first used in 1911 to describe symptoms of schizophrenia. It was not until 1943 that Leo Kanner repurposed the term to identify the condition we recognize today. In the 1950s, Bruno Bettelheim began to spread Kanner's ideas, but it would be years before there was any widespread acceptance.

Barb and Ruth agreed we would work in the same way: from conversations with Barb, as well as with Ruth and their mother, Mrs. Moran. We also used the detailed notes Mrs. Moran wrote for a psychiatrist on Barb's development from birth through her early years. (To protect the privacy of certain individuals in the story, names and identifying details have been changed.)

Barbara Moran is a very intelligent witness to the misdeeds that have been done in the name of helping. She is a survivor; she's been to the brink and has come back to tell us about it. Barb has an artistic spirit. From the start, she was going to do things her own way, because, as she says, other people mostly seemed boring to her. Human beings feel an urgent need to give names to things. We're hoping to gain some understanding and control in this baffling world in which we find ourselves. And so, at this point in time, the most reasonable approach seems to be to group people such as Barb in the category "autistic." Barb's story attests to the value of such an approach. But it is just as true that Barb, rather than acquiescing in varying degrees, as many of the rest of us do, to the deeply grooved path of the culture we've been born into, is one who, as an artist, set out on her own path.

Barb still spends a good deal of time trying to express what has happened to her and how it made her feel. She imagines how things might have gone better for her — even to the point of mapping what is currently understood onto situations she was forced to live through in the past. She's still reeling from the major experience of her life: the world's colossal misunderstanding of who she is.

I'll leave the theories to the scientists and researchers. But for what it's worth, here's how I've come to think about who we all are and what and how we learn.

Maybe you've read or heard something about physicists

speculating about dimensions in addition to the four we know (length, width, depth, and time); postulating a universe—or many universes—constructed of strings rather than particles; conjecturing about neutrinos and dark matter and probability.

My idea may seem a bit "out there" too.

Suppose one were to view the growth of our understanding of the universe, and ourselves in relation to the universe, as lying along a continuum. A great many of us learn a great many of the same sorts of things (language, bodily movement, social interaction, etc.) at the same stages in our childhood development. And together we've decided that what and how and when most of us learn constitutes a standard against which any other method of learning, any other time frame, or, indeed, any other content will be considered not just different, but deviant. (As to that other content, we'll come to that...)

Consider for a moment a musical or a mathematical prodigy, a child who in all ways has followed his or her peers in acquiring the skills we associate with normal development, but whose lightning-fast acquisition of both understanding and proficiency in the musical or mathematical realm leaves us mystified and amazed.

In such a case, we are familiar with, are able to conceive of, that part of the range of knowledge, the content (math or music), over which such a prodigy acquires mastery. What amazes us is the speed and ease—and the breadth and depth—of the accomplishment.

But maybe what we are able to learn about the universe, i.e., the content we can conceive of acquiring, is contained within a limited range of the continuum. Maybe along that continuum there are realms of content most of us will never access. Considered clearly, what we've deemed "normal" development is an astonishing wealth of acquisition. But we never recognize it as such because most of us develop in a similar fashion. For my money, the understanding and the talent of the Barb Morans of this world simply cover a different part of the spectrum of learning.

Barb is unable to grasp (or maybe "appreciate" is a better word here) the social world we've invented for ourselves within the larger universe, in the same way people with intellectual disabilities may not grasp mathematics or the written word.

But as the physicist goes about his or her work, first theorizing about a possibility and then investigating it, we need to broaden our horizons. A popular phrase not too long ago was "paradigm shift." But what we really need to do is not to shift but simply to open our expectations. As you'll see, many people in Barb's life decided she differed too much from the norm to be acceptable. But every single marginalized, passed-over individual like Barb, possesses—I hope you'll come to believe this, as I do—exclusive treasures. With this book, Barb is inviting us to admit the possibility of those riches, to theorize about unexpected human dimensions, so we'll have a chance at discovering them.

If one begins by positing the idea that each human being is unique, then what we will find is that each individual—no matter the degree to which he or she can or cannot grasp what we have deemed the common and necessary pool of knowledge/understanding/capability—each person who comes into our lives, if we look carefully and engage fully, has learned something, has acquired something, *is* something, which she or he can in turn contribute, something which (and I have no doubt about this) can reshape our lives beyond imagining.

For many years, I've worked with and for people who have intellectual disabilities, which is still all too often called "mental retardation." Once, and only once, I heard someone compare himself to a person we both knew who had an intellectual disability.

"Aaron's just like me," this man said to me shortly after we'd met, and he went on to detail how he saw his own efforts to get control of his life mirrored in Aaron's struggles.

I was astounded. The comparison was so unassuming, so truthful, so respectful, that it was remarkably refreshing.

And so I'll borrow the phrase here: Barb's like me. We're about the same age, we were both raised Roman Catholic and decided to move on from "the Church," and we both found out only later in life that we needed to devote ourselves to our ability to make things. I respect Barb's determination and courage and perseverance immensely, and she's told me that, to her way of thinking, my "shadow has steeples."

Barb and I have had (and continue to have) frequent telephone conversations. I had question after question as I worked with the material we originally recorded, and question by question, answer by answer, we became friends. And over the years, I've come to see how the intersection of our lives has helped both of us. Still, for a long time, we found it a bit awkward to make the transition necessary to end a call—she because of her difficulty with social cues and her desire to prolong a human connection, I because of my respect for her and a reluctance to curb her enthusiasm. But we found a way to solve our little problem by calling on a common childhood experience from the 1950s. It seems right to use our little discovery here, since I've finished saying what I have to say and it's time now to get on with Barb's story. And so I'll end with this: how we learned to get off the phone and on with other things.

Me, when it really was time for us to stop talking and hang up: "Okay, okay. Say Goodnight, Gracie..."

And Barb would say, "Goodnight, George."

And we'd be home free.

Mom and Dad brought me to Menninger's in September 1961. I was ten years old.

When it was time for them to leave, instead of saying, "Please don't go," I stuck my tongue out at my parents.

It didn't make me sad. If somebody criticizes you and you're mad at them a lot, when they go away, that might be the best thing they do for you.

Anyway, I had the idea it was a boarding school, and I had met several staff people at Menninger's, and I could have said to my parents, "Well, I'm going to like these people better than you."

• • •

There were mostly boys, some teenage girls, and then there were three of us younger girls. One of the teenage girls was very fat.

I'd never seen anybody as big as this and I walked up to her and said, "Hi, Fatso."

I wasn't trying to put her down; I just thought it was interesting and cute that somebody was that big.

But I only did that a couple times, 'cause she said she'd clobber me.

• • •

The younger girls were me and Carole and Alyson, who was Native American.

Carole McAlister was nine and rather slender. Her hair was brown and she wore it in curls; they'd roll it up for her every night.

I enjoyed Carole from the very first. I liked the way she laughed.

Carole wanted Alyson to be her friend, but Alyson would some-times give Carole the cold shoulder.

And Carole would plead for her attention: "Alyson, Alyson, Alyson…"

So when Carole was trying to get attention from Alyson, I always offered her mine.

• • •

The first Sunday I was there, when we were getting up, I said to one of the staff people, "It's going to be weird going to a strange church."

That person told me that, at Menninger's, they didn't go to church.

I was surprised. My Dad had said that it would be okay for me to eat meat on Friday at Menninger's, but my parents had not said anything about going to church. I thought it was a sin to miss Mass and I felt guilty. I thought God might be mad at me if I wasn't in church. I apologized to God; I said the words in my head and some tears came into my eyes.

But I got over that in a hurry. Any regrets were gone within hours, and I never worried about it after that.

• • •

There were a lot of surprises. They didn't want me to talk about the objects I pretended were alive. But when I talked about my pretend people, Carole listened and laughed and acted interested. I was punished for laughing. They didn't think that was good for me, so they kept an eye on me and Carole, and they would separate us.

Sometimes we would just say words we thought were funny, and we would laugh. One afternoon the group went to a drive-in to get a snack. Earlier that day, I'd had a weird thought that bothered me: What if somebody offered a booger to a captive traffic light? But when I heard everybody saying "ice cream cone," I thought, *What if they had a "mucus cone"?* At first this thought bothered me too, but I kept repeating those words and eventually it made me laugh. And then all Carole would have to do is say "mucus cone" and I'd double over with laughter.

But they didn't approve of that.

They were on my case from day one. I'd get into trouble and they would make me sit idle for indefinite lengths of time, until they felt like letting me get up.

I also had some frustrating moments when I tried to tell things to the people at Menninger's and they wouldn't believe me. I remember I cried about that.

· · ·

I was allowed to draw what I wanted. Sometimes they'd take my pencils and crayons away, though—usually because I was drawing on the wall or on a pillowcase. Often, they just let me be unless I drew something that really bothered them. The one picture that made them mad was a cone with green ice cream. Someone who didn't know could have taken it for lemon-lime sherbet with lime-peel bits in it—but they knew it was a "mucus cone," full of frozen nasal secretions. That's when the package of seventy-two crayons got lost.

· · ·

But there were payoffs, too. I had a $1.50-a-week allowance, which was about six times what I got at home. And there were activities and adults to give me a lot of attention. Some of the childcare workers were just the kind of people I wanted to have for parents, and they had patience and energy.

Monday through Friday, there were three workers on duty in the morning. The school was in a different building. You got up in the morning and made your bed and put on your clothes and then you had breakfast. Each group had its own area in the dining room. And then we had a little time to kill before school started at nine. People watched cartoons if they wanted to. I remember the host for a cartoon show. He was a real person and he would do a dance and some tricks...the things clowns do. And he lip-synched this recorded song, the theme song for the show, that had a full orchestra in it—the horns blowing and all that, kind of like a circus song—about himself: his red, shiny nose and his crazy, mixed-up clothes. Whizzo the Clown: your best friend. If you were sad, he'd make you glad.

PART ONE
The Years with My Family

Me with my "skunk family" of roller skates in 1957.

CHAPTER ONE

When I Was Little

I didn't want to please anybody but myself. I knew who Mom was; it was just that I did a lot of pretending and I wanted to be someone else's kid. I thought people were wet blankets. Other people's feelings, other people's happiness—they weren't important or even real to me. All I cared about was whether I was getting what I wanted. Most of the time if somebody talked to me about something that didn't interest me, I just didn't bother to listen. I don't remember this, but when I was a young child, I didn't talk much and my parents wondered then whether I was aware of anything at all, because I didn't respond to people the way they thought I should—I never looked at people. That's what Mom said.

We moved to Omaha, Nebraska, when I was three, to a fairly large house with a big yard on a corner lot. This house had front and back stairs. I counted the steps and then said, "The front stairs have twenty-one steps. The back stairs have seventeen steps. I like the twenty-one better: They have carpet and they're not slippery."

When I was little, I could have pointed to colors on a color chart that to me matched songs. I didn't see the colors when I heard the song; it was just that the song sounded like the color green, or blue, or red. But I soon realized that, when I tried to explain this, no one understood what I was talking about.

Once, I learned a new word and I forgot it. I couldn't understand how you could learn something and then not know it later. I thought when you learned something, you'd always know it. I was only around four years old and I had no comprehension of forgetting before that day.

I spent time with my brothers and sisters, but mostly I was doing my own thing. It seemed to me that other people were getting what they wanted, but because my wants were different, somehow they were inferior. When I was by myself, though, I was in a good mood. I could at least entertain myself, and I didn't realize there was anything wrong.

• • •

Mrs. Moran, for a psychologist
Born 5/29/51 Mitchell, S. Dakota
Breech; short labor; no complications
Mother 44 at birth
Bottle-fed
Sat up 8-9 mos.
Walked 17 mos.
Speech delayed compared to others in family
...the youngest of seven children...In infancy not responsive to attention. Seemed not as alert as siblings were...As a baby in play pen and creeping stage played with what was within reach. If dropped or lost never fussed or tried to regain it but turned to something else ...

As soon as walking fond of books.

...Between two and three did much drawing with whatever was at hand, during summer used a stick and drew in dirt, rubbing it out and drawing the same thing again and again.

...at three she distinguished between hexagons and octagons... When taken to see a new baby, she casually looked at the baby then examined the crib and said, "Terry's crib has 12 bars; mine only has 11." As soon as we reached home she went upstairs to check and told me she was right.

...Good vocabulary...no baby talk, but didn't converse—repeated what was said to her ...

...Discipline has never been a problem with the others. With Barbara nothing worked...Until recently didn't seem to realize that her behavior was different than other children her age. Quite troubled by it now...Loneliness seems to be a part of the picture. Has been quite upset if one animal was alone: always wanted two turtles, two pigeons, two cats, two dogs, saying they'd be unhappy alone ...

No enthusiasm for any special person, as though family and strangers were alike. If we were out in front of the house she might take the hand of anyone who passed and walk down the street with them. Would join any other family group when at the beach or on a picnic—even pick up their food. She would walk right across people lying on the beach just as though they were logs. In contrast to this vague attention to people she paid minute attention to detail of things in which she was interested. When taken to a restaurant, constantly on the move to see this and that—to such an extreme that we about gave up trying to take her places except where she could be active ...

• • •

I thought animals were prettier than people because they had fur. They were better to touch too. I didn't like to touch other people's skin; it felt like rubber to me. Different types of clothing just did not feel right. I didn't like that wet, sticky feeling you get when you wear certain kinds of clothes; I didn't like tight clothes that had no "give," such as tapered slacks or a dress with a narrow waist. I liked to have a loose top on and nothing underneath, because then I didn't feel that stickiness as much. In the summertime, we went barefoot a lot, and if I wasn't wearing shoes very much and then I put them on, I felt like my toes were squished together.

At times, some household objects would look to me like they had private parts, like they had vaginas. And I would have dreams about somebody molesting the objects. These bad thoughts were intense and I was preoccupied with them. Usually I didn't have them, but when I did, they could last for days. Not knowing any other word for what I was feeling, I would say I was "sad." But I felt I couldn't tell anybody about these thoughts and dreams. I just couldn't.

My folks took me to church every week at the cathedral. With the Latin Mass, I couldn't understand a thing they said. I simply couldn't sit still and be quiet for an hour. One time I had a fantasy while we were at church: What if the church would get up and walk someplace and put itself down somewhere else? And people would come out and not know where they were. It was just sort of a passing thought, but that was about the time I started to see how certain buildings, like capitol buildings, looked like people.

As I got older, I knew I was not like my sisters, and it grieved me. Most of my family always wanted me to do something that would please them. The only one who would ask me questions about what I was doing when I played was Ruth. When Ruth and I slept in the same room, one morning Ruth said the cathedral's birthday was coming and we should buy a present. Then we discussed what we'd get her for her birthday.

● ● ●

Ruth

My mother used to spend a lot of time with Barbie and read to Barbie a lot. I have many, many pleasant memories of my mother coming in before bed and reading us a chapter out of a book—she did that with all of us.

Barbie liked to dictate stories. Before she knew how to write, she would just tell stories to my mother and my mother would write the words. Barbie would tell her where to leave spaces and she would go back and draw pictures. My mother would cut up grocery bags, do the stories on them, and then they would be stitched together with thread or stapled to become little books. The characters in Barb's books were personified objects. She wrote books about little submarines, kitties, or her skates.

My father was a quiet, contemplative type. A nice person, he was always there, and supportive in a reserved kind of way. We all had our educations paid for. But he did not support any questioning of religion or doing anything "unchristian." For instance, gossiping—we never had open discussions at our dinner table about other people or families. We didn't complain about our teachers. Teachers, sisters, and priests were, in my father's opinion, always on the right side. If there was a conflict with one of them, you could bet you were on the wrong side. But other than that, he was a good, orderly, and gentle man.

CHAPTER TWO

Gas Pumps, Geysers, and Traffic Lights

To me, ordinary people were boring. I did like my brothers and sisters and friends of the family, but I couldn't understand any of them and they didn't understand me. I was driven into a world of daydreams because I had no way to communicate the only thoughts I could have. I never really liked the way people looked, and that had a lot to do with it. Objects just looked and felt better to me. It seemed there was nothing I could think—let alone say—that anyone wanted to hear. I pretty much had to be by myself to do things I wanted to do.

I knew people just didn't understand me. I was often lonely, and people were a disappointment. I wanted to be around someone who understood. I wanted to think someone felt like I did. I could imagine certain kinds of people I wished were in my life: people who were pleasant to look at and touch; people who made me feel safe and welcome; people I could trust not to hurt me; people who'd be there for me. And so I pretended objects were human. I enjoyed my pretend friends; they made me feel less empty.

In the early Fifties, when gas pumps had the lamps on top, I thought they looked like they could be alive and that they were cute. I was also attracted to capitol buildings; they looked like someone sitting down with the dome as the head. The Field Club where we went swimming then had a fountain in the full-sized pool, and it looked like it was alive because it just stood there in the water like a person would. I drew a picture of it with chalk on the wall in our garage. Watching *The Ruff and Reddy Show*, I became fascinated with a cartoon submarine. I thought of this type of thing as half-ship, half-animal. I also liked the TV towers in Omaha. The ones for Channel 3 and Channel 6 were the parents. The other one, the "weather tower" for Channel 7, had lights on it: red for warmer, white for cooler, green for the same. If rain were forecast, they would flash the lights. I thought of this tower as the child who wore a jacket that lit up. When I was in kindergarten, I liked the huge vent pipes on the roof of the school. They were curved at the top and I named them Larry and Flora.

I talked to Christmas trees. I liked to touch the branches and I would pull on them sometimes, so I accidentally tipped our tree over nearly every year when I was little. I would get too attached, and it was hard to see the tree go after Christmas.

We had a set of wooden building blocks. I took a certain number of blocks and named them after people in the family. Five big ones represented the older people: my brother John, sister Marty, and brother David, who were almost like adults to me, and then Mom and Dad. And four small ones represented the smaller people: Catherine, Dorothy, Ruth, and me. I could tell which one was which by the grain of the wood.

After building blocks, I played with roller skates the way Dorothy and Ruth played with dolls. Mom told me I couldn't have the regular skates, because my brothers and sisters were still using them, but I could do whatever I wanted with the keyless skates. I found some of those down in the basement behind the furnace room. I named them Tidish, Two-eared, Berings, Matilda (after the Harry Belafonte song), Alice, Zippy, and Pindin. Zippy, Pindin, and Berings were boys and the others were girls. I called them my skunk family. Skunks were furry and like cats. I didn't know until later that skunks are also big stinkers. I'd line them all up in front of the TV in the afternoon and we'd watch cartoons. I was their mom. I put out food and water for them. I'd wrap old rags and cloth strips around them like clothes and put them to bed in the doll crib next to my bed. I guarded them the way a mama bear would guard her cubs—if anyone mistreated them, I'd get mad. I played with my skates for years, until the one I considered my favorite fell apart. I lost interest right away then.

• • •

I liked the idea that I could make a mark and have it look like something. As a young child, I only drew the basic shape of a swing, because that was all I could draw that looked like something. As soon as I was able to draw other things, I did.

I remember for a while when I drew people, I drew them like my blocks: I liked the way the blocks looked. The blocks were simpler. People were just too complicated.

I drew the things I wanted to see, the kinds of things I liked looking at—objects as persons—because otherwise I couldn't see them. I wanted to be able to have an image in front of me of a better world, because I didn't think the one I was in was good enough. I drew even when nobody else looked at the pictures.

I'm glad I could draw what I wanted to when I lived at home. I always wished I could share those things with other people. But when I drew, people still didn't get it.

I liked to draw because it gave me a sense of control. On paper, I could see what I wanted to see. I drew the world as I wanted it to be. Drawing is like talking. I could speak my own language; I could show what words couldn't say.

• • •

When we went to Denver, Mom and Dad just happened to drive into a motel called The Branding Iron; it even had a logo. I had seen someone use a branding iron on *The Ruff & Reddy Show* and I'd decided I liked branding irons, so I cut pieces of cardboard and taped them together to make a branding iron. I named him Brandy and took him with me when we went to dinner.

Later on, we got a radio-phono, and when you adjusted it just right, part of it looked like a human eye. When you tuned it, the eye would be closed. I drew pictures of it. I liked the record album covers and I'd put them up on the window sill so they could watch people outside. This certainly bothered everyone, because records have to be handled carefully. But I never broke any LP records.

On a day trip to Colorado Springs when the geysers in Yellowstone went off, they looked almost solid to me, the way clouds look, and I thought I could see faces in them too.

Also in Colorado Springs they had some really cute traffic lights—four-way lights hanging from wires: box-shaped, like three cubes stacked and all fused into one, big enough to have red, yellow, and green lights in each direction, and then of course the little visors. That's when I started liking traffic lights. Back in Omaha they had some odd modern signals I didn't like. I called them "automated." But there were also traffic lights I thought of as live—the two-ways. They were standard almost everywhere. They had two sections that were at right angles and that were attached to each other at the top and on the bottom. If you were in a convertible and you stopped for the red light, you'd be right where the hanging traffic light could look down at you, because a traffic light on a pole will look directly down in front. Or they'll watch you walking down the street, and the other ones watch you in cars. I don't know the names of any traffic lights; they're all generic to me. But I thought about them on a regular basis.

• • •

When I was five and started school, I went half-days to preschool at Duchesne. Duchesne is really a French name and it's pronounced "Du-SHEN." But Dad would sometimes pronounce it "Du-CHES-nee." I thought that was a made-up nickname, until I was able to read and see how it could be pronounced that way, and that it was Dad's sense of humor.

While my parents talked with the teacher at Duchesne for the first time, I looked at the books. I wasn't reading yet, but I could look at the pictures. I liked this one book with a scene that showed a steam engine with a face; the steam engine was being worked on (I think they were taking the smokestack off), and it was crying. My father was a doctor and I liked medical stuff, but the story also seemed to show what people in my family always denied: The fact that the engine was shown crying was a message that it was okay and natural to cry when you were being worked on.

There were plenty of books around at home, and I even had a couple of train books: *The Little Train That Won a Medal, The Little Engine That Laughed,* and *The Little Engine That Could.* I thought locomotives looked like people, and I remember sneaking downstairs after I'd gone to bed and looking at them out in the hallway in an atlas that was in the bookcase with the *Encyclopedia Britannica.*

But that book at Duchesne with the steam engine was the best. And I kept running into the kindergarten room to get my hands on it.

I couldn't sit still at school; some things just didn't interest me. I would wander off and look at things I wanted to see, like the small jungle gym in the preschool room I wanted to play on sometimes. Also in preschool I remember on Valentine's Day they had paper hats with candy hearts pasted on. I ate all my hearts, then I grabbed the hearts off other kids' hats and ate them too.

Once, when I was five, Mom said, "Barbara, I could count on the fingers of one hand the number of times you've hung your coat up in your whole life."

If I got really upset, sometimes I'd cry and whine, and not even know what was wrong. I was accused of doing it to myself, of choosing to be different. Mom yelled at me and criticized me. That made me feel guilty. I knew it wasn't my fault, but I was sure no one would have agreed.

I caused her heartache, that's what Mom said.

• • •

Mrs. Moran

About this time, she started to ask questions, especially: "What's inside of __?" Spent much time examining things with a hand lens. Often responded to a question with a question of her own regarding something she had on her mind. It was as though the question you asked her didn't penetrate and would only get answered if one made a special effort to get her attention. Now she started asking the meaning of any word used in family conversation—even quite technical terms.

One of her first intense interests was in blood and anatomy. Was always at hand when a chicken was cut up to probe and question. Once her interest was aroused she kept at one, asking questions and more questions and getting quite furious if one said, "I don't know"—until we had to buy a set of encyclopedias.

Age five: Following visits from some out-of-state friends (the people meant nothing to her), she became interested in maps. From then on, maps and the globe were her constant "toys." She carried them about with her and learned to locate all the places where the before-mentioned people lived, then other places she had heard of. Soon from the globe, she identified the continents and oceans, and then moved her interest on to the universe.

She didn't seem emotionally prepared for kindergarten. We thought it advisable to have some testing done before making any further decision as to school. We took her to Dr. Philip Boyer for psychological testing. He thought she should have psychiatric attention. Then we went to Dr. Moore, a child psychiatrist. He thought we should get her with children as soon as possible. We entered her in the Duchesne Academy in the kindergarten class, but after a brief trial, they thought it better to move her to the preschool section where she remained for the rest of the year. She didn't participate in preschool activities, playing off at the side by herself, and was difficult to discipline. She was very age-conscious, was greatly bothered that she was not with five-year-olds, and would slip over to the kindergarten at every opportunity...

Chapter Three

A Horrible Driven Feeling

When I was six, I felt like I had to keep pulling up my underwear over and over again. If I was wearing a dress, it felt like my underwear was falling off. I was at the public school in kindergarten in the afternoons. I was a little bit frustrating for the staff there, I guess, but my memory is that it was a fun year; I liked kindergarten.

But those horrible physical sensations got worse and were a source of misery for me. My parents nagged me to stop, but the pressure inside of me—a horrible, driven feeling, like I was a galley slave, except that the whip was inside me—that pressure inside was even worse than being yelled at. Nobody believed I couldn't help it.

That discomfort inside would evolve into several other odd motions that became more severe as time went by. I began to understand that something was really wrong with me.

When I was seven, because the experienced first-grade teacher had quit at the end of the year and the new teacher was inexperienced, I was transferred to another public school to go to first grade. My teacher, Miss Piper, was an older lady and she was not intimidated by problem kids; she simply ignored the odd ways I moved my head or shoulders. She was sometimes rough with me and I didn't feel comfortable with her, but she never sent me home. At the end of the school year, Miss Piper wrote a really sweet note on the report card, which I saw years later. It said I had been improving with fewer outbursts (what I'd later call "upsets") and she thought the next year would be better.

• • •

I was so restless I would squirm for hours when I went to bed; my legs just wanted to run down the street. I was given Atarax to make me "feel better." But I drove myself and everybody else crazy. Mom was continually on my case.

"Barbara!" she would say. "What are you doing to yourself?"

I didn't want to do all that stuff. I remember being frustrated all the time and not being able to do anything about it. It made Mom very upset, and that made me feel so helpless. Dad didn't fly off the handle over anything, as he was very easygoing. But he had to work full time at the hospital, so he wasn't around except for evenings and weekends. My mom's discouragement, my sensitivity to pain of any kind, and the fact that I cried a lot and believed other people usually didn't—all this made me believe I was inferior to the rest of the family. None of my sisters or my brothers was like me. No one was. I worried about what was happening to me.

Before I started school, I'd heard someone refer to eight as "the golden age of childhood." I had previously believed Dorothy and Ruth were walking predictions of what I would become when I got older. But when I turned eight, I crashed and burned. Something just went wrong in my body during that summer, and there's no way of knowing what made it happen then.

I started making a "putt-putt" sound with my lips. I managed to keep quiet during church on Sundays, but only from fear of what they'd do to me if I didn't. After church, I would be twice as noisy. It really upset Mom and she was often furious with me, or at least it seemed that way. I felt abandoned, betrayed, and scared—like I had this monster within that provoked my mom.

Having big upsets and crying easily—I could no longer blame how I was on being little. I was not becoming like my sisters had been at that age. No one else had the need to keep moving some part of their body. Other people seemed to feel comfortable in their bodies. My body didn't feel right.

Our vacation the summer before to Denver and Yellowstone Park had been the happiest time of my childhood, and my parents had planned another trip for two weeks in August. The first night we stayed in Kearney, Nebraska. I was making my "putt-putt" sound and I felt very helpless and out of control. The second night, in Loveland, Colorado, it was so bad that Dad took me out of the restaurant and back to the motel room.

I cried a lot, because it hurt so much inside.

After that Mom kept reminding me, "Barbara, I could take you back home on the train and the others could go on without us ..."

The third night, we rented a cabin near a lake. I'd been licking my lips and, because of the wind outside and the dry air, they'd gotten chapped. They were beet red and very sore. That stopped the noises for a few days. But we had gone up to a higher altitude and now I was miserable because my ears bothered me. The next morning, I was awake before everyone else. I imagined someone camping in a cabin being taken away in handcuffs like a criminal, crying like he'd never stop. And I started crying really hard myself. That's how the day started. I felt very, very alone. It made me feel terrible to have the "bad habits" and to feel driven by a strange bad feeling that was relieved only by making the noises. It wore me out, and it hurt so much to be making people mad.

Luckily, because I had stopped making noises, there was a little less tension. On Sunday in Denver we went to church at the cathedral. The inside of a cathedral felt oppressive to me: You sat there doing time while the priest on the platform said Mass in a foreign language with his back toward the audience. And if your view of the front was obscured by a pillar, what you heard sounded like disembodied voices.

Two weeks later, when school was about to start, I started making a kind of barking sound, with air going inward instead of out. My family called this an "Urk." This noise was even louder than the other one and I was really scared. I thought I could hurt myself. Crying and making that noise at the same time, I started to wonder if I risked choking to death.

I said I was afraid I'd swallow my tongue.

And Mom said, "Go ahead and swallow it."

It sounded to me like she was saying, "I don't care if you live or die."

I went to bed crying and Dad came in and reassured me I couldn't swallow my tongue.

• • •

On Labor Day, there was a carnival at the seminary where my brother David had started school. My sister Marty said if I could keep quiet for an hour, she'd give me a whole bunch of pennies she'd been tossing in a container. And in the afternoon with Mom, I did keep quiet for an hour and it was hard. I barely managed it. But in the end, I had to start making the noises again and I was kept at home from that carnival.

If I'd had my way, I would not have been making noises of any kind. I felt very alone and trapped and ashamed of this ugly problem that I couldn't control and that no one else had.

When school started, I was a bigger misfit than before. My noises scared some of the other children, and one little girl even cried.

Then in October there was a school carnival, but I wasn't going to get to go. I remember Mom scolding me about the noises. She even flicked her finger poking me in the mouth.

She said, "Barbara, it's those noises you make that are preventing you from going to the carnival. There are all the tickets we bought. These unused tickets should be a reminder to you …"

That November, I ran a low fever for nearly a month, and on Thanksgiving, Dad decided to draw a blood sample. The syringe looked huge to me and I couldn't hold still. He had to use both my arms to get the sample. After that, I drove one girl at school crazy, forever grabbing her arms. I was very out of control. It was the crying I really felt ashamed of since in my family, people didn't cry; it was considered immature.

By April, they'd had all they could take of me, and I was kicked out of second grade. I knew that didn't happen to other little girls, and I felt like a failure. Even though I hated school and was relieved to not have to go, it was a really dark day for me. I thought I had really let my Mom down.

• • •

Mrs. Moran

The year she entered second grade, I tried to explain the problems—the nervous twitchings, chewing up her pencils, jerking her head, and the noises she started making at the end of the summer. And, though both teacher and principal were willing to listen, they were both inexperienced and it was more than they could understand. I arranged for them to have a conference with Dr. Moore, but even so they still didn't understand. Second grade was very difficult for Barb. The more tense she became, the worse the noises. By the spring, the noises had stopped, but they'd been replaced by a jerking of the arms severe enough to interfere with the use of a pencil. And then there was nail biting and head jerking, and a little hop every few steps. All of these manifestations of tension caused them to terminate her schooling in April. By this time, she was reading very well and was interested in books such as Toby Tyler, Alice's Adventures in Wonderland, Pinocchio, *and* Charlotte's Web, *and disliked the stories about Dick and Jane that they were reading in school. She was doing rather poor second grade work but ranked near the top of her class on the standard test just before they dismissed her.*

• • •

By the time I was nine, I had become more irritable than ever, blowing up over the smallest things. I felt a strange anxiety inside and I was often in tears if someone merely raised their voice at me. At first, I thought I was reacting to their anger. Soon I knew I was having a problem with sound. Any loud person nearby or just a voice on TV or in a movie would bother me and I cried.

And then one day right after my oldest brother, John, and his wife had a baby, my niece let out a real loud wail.

And I started crying.

That really surprised me. The sound of a baby had never bothered me before. I was reacting just to noise even if nobody was mad at me.

I didn't try to avoid the baby then. Except for that one time, I was okay with the baby. But I wondered if I'd completely fall apart someday. I knew I wasn't doing anything to myself. But I was not like anyone else I knew or had even heard about. I remember thinking, "Why am I so different from everybody else? Why do I get upset so easily and cry and feel miserable for hours?" It seemed unfair: Everybody else was okay—and I wasn't. I was unhappy, overly sensitive to pain, and just didn't feel right in my body. Other people didn't have to jerk-jerk-jerk all day long—keeping their head or their neck or some other body part moving—to relieve an unpleasant sensation. I knew something was desperately wrong, and it was getting worse all the time.

• • •

Dad taught me some catechism and I had my first confession. The monsignor gave me a pink rosary. Mom bought me a white dress and veil for my First Communion. Taking Communion made church a little easier to accept, because I could get a break when I got out of my seat.

Dad always had religious literature around. I remember reading in *The Lives of the Saints* about how the martyrs would "joyfully await their crowns" as they were being tortured. And the book would describe in gruesome detail how they were put to death.

I got curious about Our Lady of Fatima. Three children in Fatima, Portugal, saw an apparition they thought was the Virgin Mary. The Mary apparition told them to say the rosary and "make sacrifices." They were shepherds and tended sheep together alone with no adults. Their parents sent ample food and water, but they stopped eating and even drinking during the day. These visits from the apparition went on for about six months, until one day it appeared to them like the sun danced in the sky. The children began to act very disturbed. They began abusing their bodies. One girl tied a rope about her waist in such a way that it hurt her. The younger of the two girls became run-down, developed a severe infection, and was dead within a year. The boy didn't survive into adulthood either. The older girl became a nun and lived a normal life span.

After hearing the Fatima story, I began to bite the little bead-like bumps off my tongue to make it bleed. Having so much guilt and shame, I had the idea that if I could bleed—and not cry—it would please God.

• • •

My parents found a tutor for me at the college where my older sister went. She was a chemistry teacher, a nun, and she used to help anyone who came to her for help. She'd give me homework and Mom would tell me we could play a game after I'd done my assignments.

To get to the college where I was tutored, Mom drove a certain route because it had less traffic. I liked this route because there were two hanging traffic lights at one place where we turned.

The teacher worked with me for an hour a day. By the end of the summer I was nine, I was ready for fourth-grade work, so I was at the proper level for my age.

• • •

One day in May 1961, Mom and Dad said, "We're going to Topeka for a week."

It was to meet some doctors. I'd be there for a whole week with just Mom and Dad, and without my sisters.

The whole thing seemed to happen out of the blue. I really objected: I didn't want to be alone with Mom and Dad for a week.

And at the evaluation, here I was one little girl meeting four different men one on one. I felt small and helpless and scared.

I knew there were people watching me through one-way glass and I just felt violated. The psychologist made no attempt to win my trust or ensure my cooperation so he'd know I was giving my answers on the tests honestly. He did the ink blot test. And then he showed me pictures and had me tell stories. And I just made up ridiculous stories. Then there were some really obvious questions, and I gave a lot of silly answers as a way of being uncooperative and stubborn. I certainly knew old ladies weren't little boys.

I didn't realize they wouldn't recognize my silly answers as rebellion. They took this answer and all the other things I said at face value.

CHAPTER FOUR

Dr. Horowitz, Alias "Frank Sinatra"

When I met Dr. Horowitz at Menninger's for my evaluation, his voice reminded me of Frank Sinatra. I'd heard an ad on the radio with Frank Sinatra's "talking" voice. Back in Omaha they'd had the first "top 40" radio format in the country in the early Fifties. KOIL-AM (1490) was the station I listened to. We had a radio in the kitchen. And when I was not in regular school anymore and had a lot of time to kill, whenever I did stuff in the kitchen, I had it on. When I played in the living room, I listened to KOIL in there too. And in the car when Mom took me to tutoring, I wanted the radio on.

That year, I began to like disc jockeys. I knew their names and to me they were a breath of fresh air in a really stuffy world. They were always friendly and cheerful, never a harsh word. I really needed someone like that in my life. If you had imagination, the men on the radio could look any way you wanted them to. Years later, since I liked the way bishops and cardinals dressed, I imagined the DJs wearing prelate-type cassocks with red sashes.

I nicknamed Dr. Horowitz "Frank Sinatra." But I neglected to tell him why; I had no idea that what I said could be taken the wrong way. I had never heard of fantasy vs. reality, or of anyone "losing contact with reality." I knew nothing about that. I just knew I was meeting people and they were asking me questions. I didn't know what they were going to do with all that stuff. I didn't even know what mental illness was…This whole world—to me it was totally unfamiliar.

● ● ●

When the week was over and we were driving back to Omaha, Mom said, "Would you ever want to go to Topeka to live?"

I thought she was talking about down the road, when I was grown up. But one morning in August I was sitting in the kitchen eating Wheat Chex, and that's when she told me I was going to the Menninger Clinic.

Initially, I didn't want to go and I protested.

Then Mom and Dad shared things with me out of the brochure. They never let me look at the brochure, but they read parts of it to me.

So after hearing a little bit about what the place was like, I decided I wanted to go. It seemed like it really had a lot to offer. I liked all the different things kids got to do, like going to parks and swimming at the YWCA, and I remembered some of the people I'd met besides the doctors. In fact, I was really eager, even looking forward to it.

I didn't sense any tension at all; I didn't realize what everybody else was feeling. Somehow, Mom managed to conceal all her grief.

• • •

Mrs. Moran

There was no other alternative that we could see anywhere. It was a no-win situation. We thought it was essential that she be back in school and Menninger's sounded so good to us...Dr. Moore said, "It is absolutely imperative to get her into a residential situation." And there were only two places, one in Pennsylvania and Menninger's, and Menninger's had about the best reputation you could have and it was also close enough to home so that we felt that we'd be able to visit her. You still thought you were doing the best that you possibly could do and you didn't know what else you could do. Of course, we had no idea that she'd be gone that long...

• • •

Ruth

All the energy that went into all the small tasks of daily living—a tremendous amount of energy had to be channeled toward Barb. Here was a child who simply was not going to follow a single rule. Couldn't come to the dinner table at the right time; couldn't sit there; couldn't eat like the rest of us; couldn't engage in conversation. There was difficulty with every single thing there was to do. In getting dressed: Her clothes didn't feel right. At bath time: She hated getting her hair washed. With her long hair: She hated getting it brushed; she didn't want anyone to touch her hair or comb it.

But it wasn't always difficult. Before she left, when my older brothers and sisters used to bring their dates over, a lot of times Barbie was real entertainment for everyone. She was a fascinating child, spouting all these facts—she was pretty delightful with all these things she knew. The stressful times happened when Barbie wasn't in a good mood, or when we tried to get her to conform, or to do something she didn't want to do—like wearing shoes she didn't want to wear, or getting dressed, or eating. And all of that very much fell not to us, not to Barb's brothers and sisters, but to my mother.

My parents weren't concerned about her intelligence. They were concerned that there would be no place for her in the world unless she could go to school and learn to be like everybody else. And if she couldn't learn how to be like everyone else...I'm sure that "what if" was pretty frightening to them, so they really wanted to put all their efforts into where they could put her so that she would learn social skills and get an education.

I know the stress level in our household was very, very high.

I remember the day Barbie's suitcase was being packed. We did know she was going to go to this place in Kansas, but I don't think that we were too aware of what the place was. I guess we didn't really know how to think or feel. It's very difficult to see one of your family members be taken away. Then when she was gone and my parents were back home, my mother spent a lot of time crying—which I don't believe she did beforehand, or in front of Barb. It was a very difficult decision for them to make, I'm sure. But they simply didn't have another idea.

PART TWO

Menninger's: The Hospital

My pre-admission Polaroid photo taken at Menninger's
in Topeka, Kansas, May 1961.

CHAPTER FIVE

At First It Seemed Like a Great Place

There were twenty-eight of us: the oldest boys on the third floor, the smaller and middle-sized boys on the second floor ("middle-sized" was the word they used for the younger teenage boys), five older girls in their teens, and three of us younger girls. Most girls had their own room.

At first, it seemed like a great place. Our rooms were well-furnished, and everyone had nice clothes and an allowance. We had parties, picnics, access to a gym, tennis courts, and baseball diamonds, and there were two paid activities offered every week. There was even a pond that had been stocked with fish.

The staff wore their own clothes and there were enough of them to give individual attention, and I was able to get plenty. We generally had three childcare workers on duty when there was no school, sometimes even four.

We got up at 7:30 every day. The childcare workers typically would accompany us over to what they called the Southard School. I was in fifth grade, but I had enough smarts that they gave me sixth-grade work and then they put me in seventh grade the next fall. We had small classes and we went all day and then just in the mornings in June and July.

The first class I was in had three boys. I was the only girl. But I liked the teacher, Clement Corgan, who was just a pleasant person to be with.

One boy in the class was named Jack. He absolutely did not want to be called "Jackie," and he kept thinking someone was calling him "Jackie" even when they weren't.

He'd say, "Stan teased me! Stan teased me!"

I never heard Stan say anything.

But Dennis, Jack's roommate, did tease him a lot.

Dennis would say, "Jackie-Jackie-Jackie-yie-yie-yie …"

I'd only been there a couple days when Jack told me, looking at Dennis, "You see that boy down there? He's got a widow's peak. I want you to pull it."

I wasn't going to do that!

Dennis had a little balsa-wood airplane out in the hall. I didn't realize it was there and I accidentally stepped on it. Dennis kicked me. I don't remember exactly what the staff did with him, because he wasn't in my class, but they wouldn't have allowed somebody to kick and get away with it.

Another boy was Timothy Reston. At first, I thought he was really smart because he did well in spelling. But when he got glasses and the teacher told him to clean his glasses, he took them off and tried to clean them with his fingers. For one assignment, we had to stand in the front of the room and give a talk about something we'd studied. When it was Timothy's turn, Mr. Corgan said, "It's up to you: You can have your notes or leave them on your desk."

Timothy couldn't make up his mind whether to leave the notes on the desk or carry them with him. He got so frustrated he finally said, "I feel like crying." I thought that was so cute!

It shocked me that some of the kids at Menninger's used profanity. I knew you weren't supposed to take the Lord's name in vain. I had no idea what those other words meant, but they sounded interesting.

I doubt Timothy was used to hearing people cuss either. One day he was sitting in class, thinking out loud, and he said, "I wish there was a book called *How to Cuss: Cussing Made Easy*." Once another boy, who was a couple of years older than me too, like Tim, got frustrated with his math. And I heard him say, "Shit, fuck, BM, penis." It was cute, I thought.

The teacher went out of the room to phone to have them come and take that boy back to the unit. We were sitting at our desks, and while Mr. Corgan was gone, another boy named Mark, who had just come to Menninger's, said, "Fuck a duck ..."

Then he said to me: "Pull your pants down."

That was a little bit scary. I don't think he was actually wanting me to do it, but just wanted to talk dirty.

• • •

Carole had gone to regular kindergarten when she still lived at home with her parents. She told me her brother Billy never talked. I think Carole must have been two or three when Billy was born. Her other brother, Ronnie, was four or five years younger than her. I think the reason Carole wound up at Menninger's was because her parents couldn't handle taking care of her and her youngest brother. Both Carole's parents had severe problems. Her Dad had been in the Marines and had suffered trauma in World War II. He was a veteran on disability. He met her Mom when they were both patients at Menninger's. Both her parents drank and abused drugs; she had at least two aunts and I think both her grandmothers were alive, but none of her rich relatives was willing to raise her. Carole was not even six when she entered Menninger's. Ronnie was the lucky one. He stayed at home and went to regular school.

For about three years before I arrived, I think Carole was the only little girl at Menninger's. The other girls must have been at least twelve or thirteen. Having no other girls to play with, Carole was sad and she told me she cried a lot. She was not punished much before I came, but I don't think anyone took her feelings seriously.

About a year before I arrived, another little girl came to Menninger's. Carole was eight then and Alyson, the other girl, ten. Alyson played with Carole some, but as I saw it, Alyson was stubborn and sometimes Carole would literally beg for her attention. Carole was very needy because she'd been deprived of access to girls her age. Menninger's called her sadness and her neediness "a problem with being liked" and said it was part of her illness, a psychiatric problem.

But Carole was a strong little girl. I met her when she was nine and I was ten. She'd been at Menninger's for four years and was still able to feel and laugh and cry. Even though she was at Menninger's in time for first grade and she was smart and eager to learn, Carole was one grade behind when I came.

Carole thought I was a fun girl—she laughed at my jokes and she could say things to make me laugh. I never connected well with the other girls. If Carole had not been there at Menninger's, I don't know what I would have done.

But the staff decided our friendship was not appropriate and they fought us day and night.

Because of me, Carole was put into long timeouts all the time. I was too, of course, but I got her into trouble like no one else did.

If we misbehaved at bedtime—and that just meant if we annoyed the staff—they sometimes made us get up half an hour early to sit in the hall. But for me, sitting in the hall wasn't any worse than lying awake in bed. Getting-up time was 7:30 a.m., way too late for a 9 p.m. bedtime. I didn't need as much rest as they thought I did. I was always awake for a long time—thirty minutes to nearly an hour—before they let me get up. On weekends there was no staying up later, but they still made us stay in bed an extra hour on Sunday mornings. It was frustrating to spend time in bed having to be idle and quiet. To me, that was like several hours of timeout scheduled in the day every day when I hadn't done anything wrong!

Soon they decided Carole and I had to be apart unless someone was watching us. Since we slept in the same room, they put someone in the room with us at bedtime, to spy on us until we went to sleep.

• • •

One of the childcare workers was Jill Perry. She was tall and slender with dark hair. I liked her at once. She seemed like the kind of person I would have followed out of the grocery store. She was young and sweet, a very gentle person who cared about your feelings and wanted you to be happy and to feel safe. She never raised her voice or acted harshly. When I complained about loud noises bothering me, Jill would explain to me that there were other people at Menninger's who were sometimes bothered by loud noises too.

I liked most of the childcare workers. A number of them were very affectionate with me. Belle started working there about a month after I came—a wonderful, older, grandmother-type lady who let me sit on her lap.

Some of the male workers were stricter and they used to tell the gentler childcare workers that they were spoiling me.

We went out riding in the van and I wound up sitting next to Dennis, one of the boys who was around my age. They drove us on some bumpy roads out in the country and Dennis said, "I feel like my stomach's out there on the road." I imagined stomachs all over the place: stomachs swimming in the farm ponds, stomachs in barns, stomachs everywhere. And I laughed. Carole started laughing too, and she didn't even know what I was laughing at. When we got back, the male worker made me sit on the couch in the upstairs hallway. And he made Carole sit on the top bunk in the bedroom. I didn't think I'd done anything wrong. I went down the hall and smiled at Carole, sitting on the top bunk in her stocking feet. The male worker told me to get back out there in the hallway, but I went down the hall for one more peek and he grabbed me and swatted me a few times.

Sure, some people at the school were strict, but I was in Topeka, and Mom and Dad were in Omaha. They couldn't pick on me or criticize me, and I wasn't angry at them anymore. I remembered my folks, but the people I was around were more real to me and I just didn't think about my family much anymore. Beginning the first day I was there, my Mom wrote me regularly, several times a week. But I was just too lazy to write letters. I hardly wrote to anybody.

I was in Menninger's old house in the city for about two months. I was the last child admitted to the old house. When we moved to Menninger's new buildings in November, we became five groups: the teenage boys on the hill in Hilltop and Hillside (there was also a small unit called Hillcrest for difficult kids). In my building was Sunrise Hall, for younger teen-age boys; Whitney Hall, for the older girls; and Children's Corner, for the younger kids. I helped think of that name, brainstorming with the activity director before we moved to the new facility.

Each unit had a playroom downstairs (our unit had a "home-bound classroom" downstairs too), and upstairs were the living room and bedrooms. Everyone used the dining room in our building.

For a while I felt like I wasn't even with the right species. Some of the kids in my group did not talk. Donnie didn't do anything except swing his arms back and forth and rock and go, "Hnnn..." They told me he could talk but didn't want to. He didn't even ask to go to the bathroom, and sometimes he'd wet himself. But I thought he was just very keyed up, not unaware.

Tad wasn't able to talk either. He and Donnie were taught in the homebound classroom. Someone worked with Tad one on one; he was learning how to write. He used some signals for the days of the week. And if he had to go to the bathroom, he would touch his crotch and make a "b" sound: "Buh, buh ..." But Tad would have given his teeth to talk! He got fascinated with shopping, and the lady who taught him took him to the grocery store. Then they put paper all over the walls and Tad drew shelves on the paper with a box of cereal that read: "Kellogg's BM Flakes" — making fun of bran flakes, because they used to call it "the laxative cereal." I thought that was really cute. But most of the other kids were afraid of Tad because sometimes he kicked people, and he was a pretty good size. Tad's teeth enamel wasn't all that strong, so he wasn't allowed to eat sweets of any kind. When we went to a clinic to get the polio vaccine, Dr. Annette Thomas (the group doctor for the younger kids) gave Tad his sugar cube. Back on the unit later, he gagged himself and kept saying something that sounded like, "Teeth, teeth ..." like: "Sugar's bad for my teeth! And I ate a sugar cube. Oh, no!"

Another guy, Arthur, who went to regular classes at Menninger's, would sometimes take stuff that was important to me and tear it up. But he loved anything that had to do with radio or TV, too; he wanted to be a television announcer. Arthur was taking meds for grand mal epilepsy, but he still had seizures. The first time I saw Arthur having a seizure, I didn't know what seizures were and it kind of looked like he was laughing or just acting weird.

For a while Menninger's had a Japanese childcare worker, who knew Japanese and Korean, and a Japanese doctor. They would get together and talk a blue streak in Japanese. It always looked to me like it made them feel like a million dollars. Arthur asked the childcare worker to teach him some foreign words. He did learn a few, and you could tell he wanted to learn more, but he had a hard time; he just couldn't remember. After a while, the childcare worker didn't want to bother teaching him anymore.

Preston was the other boy in our group. He had a collection of military stuff, toy soldiers and vehicles. He wore his hair in a crew cut and I remember he got frustrated with reading and math, and he cried easily. Preston seemed okay to me, but for a couple of months they had him restricted to his room and they wouldn't let him go anywhere.

• • •

So when we first moved to the new residence, there were seven kids in our unit: Carole and me and Alyson, and Arthur and Preston and Tad and Donnie.

All the doors in the new building had locks on them, and at first they were locking everything. When you came in from school or from an activity, first the outside door at the bottom of the stairs had to be unlocked, then the one that led to the bottom of the stairwell, then the one at the top of the stairs. They locked the bathrooms. There were locks on the closet doors. I remember coming home and I'd have to ask them to unlock the section where I'd picked the bedroom I wanted; then I had to ask them to unlock my bedroom; and then I had to ask them to unlock my closets. It was almost like a prison. Fortunately, that went on only for a short time.

I thought I'd get to play on all the grounds they had, but it didn't turn out like that. The old house in the city had been on a fairly small parcel of land, maybe two or three acres, and you could go outside and play. But the new school was on grounds that covered the area of several city blocks. There wasn't a fence or a wall around the place, and there was no way they could keep track of you. So staff had to take you outside.

I liked the way our building looked, and when I got bored and needed a new fantasy, sometimes I would start talking to it. And this one childcare worker, who was extremely strict with me, would send me inside for the rest of the day. That happened again and again.

Most little girls, one minute they can be screaming and the next minute laughing. But if something happened that made me upset, I'd be miserable the rest of the day. Sometimes it was for no reason; I just went through spells of it. My parents never told me it was okay to have emotions. At Menninger's they tried to tell me crying was okay. I had trouble believing that.

I've always had a desperate need for touch, but often it just didn't feel right. I couldn't accept it from people I had a conflict with. Closeness was just plain threatening to me, as if the other person were taking over. I thought if someone touched me, I would have to try harder to please them. So when I was upset at Menninger's, there were only certain people I wanted to be around. But I just couldn't get enough. I would want that person to talk to me and comfort me for hours. I could cry and be completely inconsolable and pester people to be right there with me.

They hired an older lady they said they thought I would like. But this lady was stricter than Belle. If she scolded me, I didn't like the sound of her voice and it made me cry.

Chapter Six

Drifting Off to La-La Land

I kept hearing the childcare workers and the doctors referring to people as "sick." They'd say we had to stay at Menninger's until we "got well." That seemed strange.

"They have no definition of what well is!" I heard one teenage boy say. You could tell he didn't consider himself sick at all.

To me, being "sick" meant having a fever. I didn't consider myself sick because my temperature was normal. But I knew something was wrong with me, and I did have a definition of "well." To me, "well" meant the ability to accept life as it happened and not get upset over little things. "Well" meant having the ability to give and take, to be able to be part of a group and contribute. "Well" meant I'd rarely feel like crying unless there was a real reason for it. "Well" meant being able to act responsibly. "Well" meant not having the need to move parts of my body repeatedly. "Well" meant tolerating pain, bouncing back after getting hurt, and not being in a bad mood the rest of the day. "Well" meant tolerating noise.

Before I went to Menninger's, I didn't think there was anything wrong with seeing objects like people, and I had no idea why anyone would object. I'd heard the words "pretend" and "make-believe play," which all children do. But I'd never heard any other word for what I did.

The terms "fantasy" and "reality" came at Menninger's. Any time I pretended something was human, they thought of me as not being "in reality," and they were against it. But I thought it was wrong for them to want me to give it up. I needed to see certain things as human in order to be happy.

I was accused of being "in my own world," as if that were actually possible. They said I was choosing to "escape into fantasy" because I didn't want to "face reality." I could not be myself; I had to be like them, a shadow of what they were, or they would not accept me in their world.

The people at Menninger's never considered that to people with imagination, reality doesn't disappear. Reality *is*. I could see it; I could hear it; it was all around. No one ever bothered to find out what I was really aware of. They never asked me to describe what I saw, to recall what happened in school or during the evening or when they made me watch a movie, to see if I actually paid attention and what I noticed. Never. It was so confusing. I knew I had problems: getting upset and crying and having to move parts of my body and all the rest. But none of this concerned them. They were too busy trying to get me to stop my "fantasies," as if they just had to stamp them out, come hell or high water. Over time, I saw that they needed to believe that what was wrong with me couldn't happen to them because they were "being good." Perhaps it made them feel safer or more stable to hold onto this belief.

I looked up "mental illness" in the encyclopedia, and schizophrenia was described in that article. There were some sub-types of schizophrenia. One had characteristics called "silliness" and "withdrawal into fantasy." There was so much talk about me being "in fantasy," that when I read that in the encyclopedia I thought, *Well, maybe I'm schizophrenic.*

They wouldn't admit it; everybody denied that they'd labeled me with anything. But they thought they had to work real hard to keep me from drifting off into La-La Land and never coming back.

One day they changed our dinner hour so all of us could see *The Twentieth Century* program on TV that featured Menninger's. Before that, I had no idea what a state hospital was. From watching that program, I learned what mental hospitals were once like, that they used to put people in restraining cages or tie them up. I realized there were really bad places where people went and stayed all their lives.

Directly east of Menninger's there were these big, spooky, prison-like buildings made out of stone. You couldn't even see them from the offices. You had to be upstairs on one of the units because they were a long way back on the property. You could tell they'd been there for a long, long time. At first, I'd wondered why the heck they were over there. That was the state hospital. There was a hill and then a children's institution and you could see the kids when they played outside on the swings. The adult hospital was farther back.

After seeing that TV program, the visible presence of the state hospital meant: "You don't clean up your act, you're coming here."

• • •

My social worker was Mr. Grey. You could make an appointment whenever you wanted to; you just asked and they arranged it. If you hadn't seen him for a while, the social worker might set up an appointment himself.

When I first got there, I never thought about how long I'd be at Menninger's. I didn't care about the future; all I cared about was whether I was getting what I wanted. Also, I had this belief in the back of my mind that when I got older, things had to get better. During the first two months I was at Menninger's, I never talked about seeing my parents. Carole didn't see her family at all. But I thought everybody went home over the Christmas holidays and the staff had the holidays off, and I assumed I would be home then. It wasn't until near December when I learned the truth: Hardly anyone went home for Christmas. I would have a visit with my parents, but not see anyone else—none of my sisters or brothers.

All I'd get is forty-five minutes with my parents in the social worker's office, forty-five minutes as a little girl being stared at by three adults. Being alone with more than one powerful person at a time was intimidating—they weren't just adults; they were also big bosses in my life, all of them.

There wasn't even a pretense of explanation such as, "We think if the visit was too long that it would possibly upset you," or, "We want to have a smooth visit, not a stormy one."

I was shocked and very disappointed. I wouldn't even get to eat a meal with them.

I knew by then, of course, that Menninger's wasn't a boarding school. I'd been taken away from my family.

When the day came for the first visit, I went to Mr. Grey's office. Mom had her arms open wide to hug me when I walked in. I'm sure Dad hugged me too. But after that, it felt uncomfortable. I had no sense of feeling loved or welcomed. I'd been separated from my parents for three months, and they seemed like strangers.

The visit was so short, and there was not time to do anything. I don't recall what we talked about. I'm sure Mom talked about what was happening at home, and I probably talked about what I was doing. My parents gave me a box of maple-sugar candy.

They were all models of "having it together" and I was the little girl who couldn't live at home. Most of the kids had been at Menninger's for over two years. Carole had been there for four, and no one was even thinking about Carole getting out in the foreseeable future. I knew it could be years before I'd go free.

That penitentiary-type visit made me feel as though I had been lied to and that I couldn't trust anyone. I thought my parents didn't cry, didn't feel fear or shame. They were strong; I was weak. They were respectable adults taking care of others. I was so inferior that I was called "sick" and had to live in a hospital. I had no idea how bad my parents felt and that they were fighting tears. Decades later, I'd learn, but if I had known it then, it would have terrified me. It already felt as though I was no longer their daughter. It would have appeared to me that they were helpless and unable to protect me from harm, and that maybe they weren't even really my parents anymore. How else could someone ration the time a little girl spends with her parents—unless they were a far higher authority? At any other time, the father would have had the final say.

Years later, Mom said my behavior during that first visit was horrible. I must have been loud and I probably did more talking than listening.

Mr. Grey tried to explain my behavior to them: "Well, that tends to happen," he said, "when people have their first visit." Years later, that's what Mom told me he said.

• • •

Mrs. Moran
We would go down and we'd have to have our conference with the social worker. The parents didn't know too much. There were no psychiatric terms mentioned; nothing was said about what the doctors thought. And that was a very difficult thing for Barb, because she said, "Everybody's looking at you and saying things about you" and they're "behind your back," so to speak. She knew that reports came in from the...I guess they called them caretakers...

One of the advantages—if you could call it that—of having Barbara in a place like that was that they had a crew that changed—so many hours on and so many hours off. At home, we had twenty-four hours of on.

We hardly ever saw anybody else. I remember seeing Carole McAlister once. And I remember another little girl saying to Barb, "Oh, here comes your big toe." Now whether the family was her big toe...I never did know quite what that meant. That's my sum total of seeing any other patient there.

CHAPTER SEVEN

You Push People Away

Everybody who lived at Menninger's had a therapist. The therapists had their offices right on the grounds and they worked from 8:30 until 5:00. My therapist, Dr. Albericht, was in the boys' building up on the hill; he was the group doctor for those older boys. Dr. Horowitz was the group doctor for the older girls in Whitney Hall, and Dr. Annette Thomas was the group doctor for the youngest kids. You saw your therapist the same time every week, and if you had a therapy appointment during the school day, you were excused from class for therapy.

I saw Dr. Albericht three times a week for fifty minutes. Back then, they all wore suits, and when I first met him, he seemed okay. I thought he knew something.

When you walked in his office, there was a chair next to the desk, his chair at the desk, a closet that had some lockers where you could keep stuff, a place for him to keep his coat, and toys. There was also a green chalkboard that was about twenty-four by twenty-four inches, and he wrote on it with yellow chalk.

At first when I went to see him, I played with the toys. One day I made a wall of blocks next to a doll on a block. I was pretending the doll was on a bed getting an EEG and the testing equipment was on the other side of the wall, as they had it at the Menninger's lab. I accidentally knocked the blocks over and I was in tears. I acted as if I had hurt myself. It was really the sound I reacted to; I was just ashamed to admit that. It would be a long time before I said anything much to any doctor at Menninger's about noise upsetting me.

When I didn't feel like playing with toys anymore, I talked to Dr. Albericht.

Shortly after we met, around Christmastime, I told him that sometimes I felt lonely.

I couldn't understand what made people angry at me, what made them criticize me. They had a list of things they said people wouldn't like about me: pretending things were people, being in fantasy, my loud voice, my talking too much, and the noises and movements I still made.

"Barbara, you push people away." That's what Dr. Albericht told me.

I didn't mean to drive people away. I didn't ask for that type of personality.

• • •

None of the younger kids went home for Christmas. Several of them didn't see their parents at all, because it was too far for their parents to travel. Carole's family lived in town, but she only spent about two hours with them at Christmastime.

When Carole's visit was over, she was crying.

"I don't like this place," she said. "I want to go home!"

When someone said, "I want to go home," sometimes one of the staff would say, "Get well and you'll get out of here."

They had a tree on the unit, and on Christmas morning they gave everybody Christmas stockings. All the kids got presents that their families provided. But I didn't write a Christmas list to my folks, so I didn't like a lot of the things I got.

Even though when I was living at home I did not look as though I was aware of other people being around, I was always the happiest just knowing my brothers and sisters were there. And now I really missed them.

I was deeply ashamed of myself because I thought I was regressing when other ten-year-old girls were really big girls. In art class when we drew and painted pictures of things we could see, I painted a picture of an infant with big breasts because I felt that even though I had big-girl breasts, I was like a baby.

At Menninger's, the kids picked on each other a lot. They would say the meanest things they could think of to each other. I did it too. But the staff didn't do much. They would just separate us for half an hour maybe.

In the spring of '62, a girl named Darlin' came to Menninger's. Darlin' was only six and a half years old, the youngest and the smallest kid in the unit. She'd had an ulcer, and back then they thought ulcers were a symptom of mental illness.

Sometimes Darlin' cried for her mom and dad. Kids would call her a baby and humiliate her. The staff winked at that; they didn't crack down on it the way they cracked down on other things.

In May, about a month after Darlin' arrived, a cute boy named Richard came to Menninger's. He had red hair and freckles, and he and Preston became friends. Richard had a toy bazooka Preston liked, and if Preston didn't do what Richard wanted, he'd say, "Okay. No bazooka."

One time, Richard drew a picture of a frog jumping into water head-first and water splashing and the frog pooping into the air.

Richard used to come up from behind and grab my breasts and say, "Bosoms! Bosoms!"

And there was a joke he told that summer:

Q: What are you doing, Mom?

A: I'm baking a cake.

Q: Can I lick the bowl?

A: No, flush it.

He was playful and full of mischief, but he also seemed to be a sensitive boy who cried when he was hurt.

Richard thought it was cute that I drew pictures of buildings. Once he asked me to draw one I liked, and he actually used the name I'd given to the building.

That summer, we went out to Topeka Funland, the amusement park, and when we came back to Menninger's, we raced back to the building before the childcare workers and ran up the stairs. The outside doors weren't locked this time. We had about thirty seconds at the top of the stairs with no staff supervision. Richard pulled out his wiener for us to admire. He was only eight years old, so his wiener was a little bitty thing. But we just loved it: We'd pulled a fast one on the staff, and we all felt very proud.

The first couple of weeks of August, they rented a campground called Camp Kiwanis near Lake Shawnee. Everybody moved out of the facility so they could do different types of jobs that couldn't be done when the kids were around, like painting or working on the water heater. At the camp, they had a one-rope swing tied in a tree with a bag of rags at the end for a seat.

"Tarzan!" Richard would say when he swung on it.

Sometimes the staff were permissive and I got to talk to the Lodge Building. And I understood what it was saying: all the kinds of things I wished people would say.

I got attached to it, and I remember I cried when it was time to leave the camp.

That summer on the last day of camp, August 14, I had my first period, and I became more anxious. I knew hormones during the little-girl-to-big-girl stage can make life stormy. For a while, it was hard to sort things out.

Several childcare workers left after that first year, and I was glad to see all of them go because they were harsh. But when Jill Perry got married and then in the fall told us she would be leaving, I tried to talk her into staying.

"Just because he's leaving town," I said, "doesn't mean you have to go."

And she said, "But I love him …"

Hey, we loved her too. Or at least I did.

Later she came back for a visit, and then I never saw her again.

CHAPTER EIGHT

Barbara, You Have to Tell Me

At Menninger's they were so strict they saw illness in everything.

I sometimes asked Dr. Albericht about it.

"Why don't I fit in?" I'd say.

Or, "How am I supposed to act in this situation?"

Or, "What's wrong with what I'm doing?"

Or, "How am I supposed to do all this right?"

Or, "How am I supposed to feel?"

Or, "How do other people feel?"

And Dr. Albericht would say, "Barbara, you have to tell *me* that."

• • •

I saw my parents for just a few hours at the end of school, and then at the end of summer. A couple hours each time. Something Mom had told me made me think that kids only stayed at Menninger's until they were twelve. I was supposed to get help, get better, and go home again.

But there were teenagers at Menninger's—as old as eighteen—people who had lived there for years.

It was sad to see September come when I was eleven. I'd been in a psychiatric facility for a year and I knew I was not getting any better. In fact, I felt like I'd only gotten sicker. Besides crying easily, getting really upset, and not being able to snap out of it, now things bothered me that hadn't ever bothered me before. Sometimes before this, thoughts I didn't ask for would come into my mind. But now I was getting thoughts I didn't want in a lot more situations, and I felt I couldn't tolerate being in those situations. I hadn't seen any of my sisters in a year, only my parents. In the fall that year, I saw the reality; that's when it hit me how serious everything was. I knew it would be a long time before I'd go home or go anywhere.

CHAPTER NINE

On Drugs

Dr. Thomas, our group's doctor, talked to us every day. And listened to us. As a group. But then each of us got to spend about ten minutes every day with her—and if we needed to talk, she would always talk to us individually. I think she really wanted to be involved; she really cared about how people felt.

She told me there was a medication she thought would make me less anxious. I have no idea if my therapist, Dr. Albericht, was in on the decision. There was no discussion. I was just told I'd get the pill.

I longed to feel, to think, and to function like an ordinary person. I didn't have the faintest idea that I could be given a pill that would make me worse.

Dr. Thomas put me on Thorazine in mid-October. I think there were a couple other kids on the unit who took it too.

Soon I started to feel tired and lethargic. When I complained about this, they started giving me Ritalin too.

I was taking 125 mg of Thorazine and a small Ritalin tablet with my morning and noon doses. When the Ritalin was first added, I felt irritable, and I said I thought the Thorazine wasn't working.

Saturday morning, the eighth day I was on the drugs, I remember sitting on the floor in the hallway by the office door. The haunting melody of "Leah" by Roy Orbison was on the radio. It was cloudy and dark, and I was feeling terrible. I was anxious. Not like the anxious you get when you're afraid of something, just a different kind of awful feeling.

That afternoon our group went to Lake Shawnee. I don't remember if Carole was sitting with me in the van, but it wouldn't have done her any good to be around me, because all the life was out of me.

Over to the east side of the lake at the playground, all the kids got out of the car and headed for the swings. Usually when we went places, I was out ten feet ahead of everyone, like a gazelle. But I didn't have that enthusiasm anymore. I was miserable. I wouldn't even get out of the car.

One of the childcare workers with us that day was Patsy. That's what everyone called her anyway; her real name was Betty Anne. Patsy was a very sweet lady in her thirties with short blond hair. She was very affectionate! I think I reminded her of her daughter. She liked to wrestle with me and hug me and kiss me.

Patsy offered to take me down to the campground so I could see my friend down there, the Lodge Building I called Robert Reynolds.

But I couldn't control my thoughts. And I felt so bad all over that I didn't want to go with her. I kept covering my head. I just wanted to crawl under a rock and bury myself. I was torn because I had really gotten attached to the building during the summer, and now Patsy was going to let me talk to it. I felt a real loss. But I just couldn't function. It was absolute torment.

• • •

In school, Clement Corgan, the teacher I had liked, was gone. I had a new teacher and it wasn't the same. Still, I was in class every day. But that changed just after my second Halloween at Menninger's, when I started avoiding school. Some classes—math, spelling, and English—generally didn't bother me, though I did have trouble reading literature or being in the library. But I had always enjoyed music, gym, history, and geography classes, and now they had become triggers for the worst anxiety. In American history I thought, *What if they used first names for city names and* *last names for state names? My name's Barbara and there's Santa Barbara in California and Santa gives people Christmas presents and I've given people stuff for Christmas before. Maybe not as much as they give me...*It would go on and on like that, and it interfered with me doing my schoolwork. In the morning, I'd get dressed and they'd give me my pills and I'd go out to the dining room. And before I'd finished eating, I would get these thoughts. We were studying Latin America, and the strange-sounding names of the countries made these nonsense syllables that I didn't ask for come into my head. And then I'd get anxious; it seemed like the thoughts themselves made me anxious. And if I moved much, I would feel even more anxious. It was a strange sensation in my body, a feeling of dread. It seemed to start at the top of my head and move down through my body. Sometimes I'd put my hands over my head. Or we'd be walking along on the way over to school and I would try to get my head under the childcare worker's arm. This was usually Virgil R. Virgil was quite gentle and caring, not as strict as the other male workers, and he let me do it.

I was the only girl in a classroom full of boys and with a male teacher. I was kind of scared and felt like I was in enemy territory, so I begged to be moved into a class with girls.

They did put me in music class with girls. It was going to be one day a week. The other day I was going to be in the music class-room by myself with just the teacher—they called her a music therapist—and no other kids.

Generally, I was okay around this teacher and in the music room. I could draw pictures or listen to records. They had a really good record collection. I could sing any song in the songbook and the teacher would sing with me. But that day the theme song of some TV show got stuck in my head and I spent the whole hour sitting on the floor crying. I really gushed. I was so wild that, to keep me from running out of the classroom, the teacher pushed the small piano in front of the door. So, I sat on the floor and cried, and she gave me a lot of Kleenex and tried to comfort me. But she had no idea why I was crying.

After that, I was always with other girls.

At the beginning when these things happened, I would think I was just having a bad day. I'd manage to make it through school, but I could hardly wait for the day to end. After that, I often had to force myself to go to classes, and then I would beg to return to the unit. I was learning practically nothing in what had been my best classes.

I also didn't want to go to the gym. I just wasn't up to it. The childcare worker wanted to make me. But Dr. Thomas told him not to make me go if I didn't want to.

I could've done embroidery or crocheting and the staff would have helped me. Or I could've read books: Southard School had a library and the English teacher at Menninger's had lots of novels that kids borrowed. But the medicine made me just too apathetic.

• • •

I've always liked music and at least they didn't try to take that away from me at Menninger's. I'm sure a lot of it is exaggerated, but I love hearing guys sing about how wonderful the world is because they've met this girl, or about crying if they've lost her. In music class, it was okay if real music was playing. I was able to enjoy that. But if no music was actually playing, and if I saw something that could create music but that was silent—an instrument that wasn't being played or a phonograph that was off—then some song would pop into my head and run through my head with intense waves of anxiety. I couldn't control any of my thoughts anymore; it was as if reality was being taken away from me. I felt out of control, like my mind had a mind of its own.

• • •

In December, another boy came to Menninger's. He was ten years old but tall for his age. Then Richard and Tad and Donnie and this new boy named Rodney Stoner were all in the large bedroom.

The boys used to talk after they went to bed, and they'd get punished for it.

Once, when Richard was being made to sit in the hall, he got mad at a childcare worker named Zach.

"You shitter!" Richard yelled at him.

Zach was the childcare worker the whole group hated. We all wanted him to be fired.

"Fucker!" Richard said.

For Christmas that year, Richard got a Chubby Checker record and everyone was doing the Twist while I sat and stared into space, too miserable to do anything.

People started to snap their fingers in my face.

"Snap out of it, Moran!" they'd say.

I guess I must have looked spaced out.

That year they decorated the Christmas tree in the living room on a Saturday morning. I was so anxious that I was unable to get pleasure from most things I'd once enjoyed. I did want to decorate my room in some way, but I didn't know how. The staff suggested pictures, but I turned that down. At that time, if I had a visual image in my mind, I didn't want to be in any room that had pictures on the wall. For instance, there were a couple of Grandma Moses prints on the wall in the dining room. And if I had a visual thought, I felt I had to go and look at each of those Grandma Moses pictures. This was a way, I thought, to try to get reality back: I had to look at something "real." The visual thought could've been anything—it didn't have to be disturbing. But then sometimes those pictures in the dining room themselves would make the thoughts start, and then I would need to look at the pictures again. If I could, I would've just taken all those pictures down. That would have gotten me out of that cycle. So I didn't want to go near that tree. That second Christmas, most of the time I felt unreal. All I wanted to do was lie on my bed and have somebody come in and sit with me.

• • •

The second time Mom and Dad came down, at the end of school, they'd taken me shopping downtown for several hours. After that, I always got to go out when my folks came to visit.

But when I asked Mr. Grey if I could spend the night with them, he said, "You don't need to spend the night with them. You have a bed here."

Then Mr. Grey left and he was replaced by Mr. Peale. When I saw my folks for a few hours the day after Thanksgiving, I asked them if they could sneak Ruth down the next time.

"Just bring her down," I said, "but don't let anybody know."

Christmastime 1962 was the first time I saw my sisters again. I would have refused to go home for Christmas; I would have gotten upset if they had tried to make me go home, because I felt so much worse. I recall that morning: While I was waiting to be taken up to meet them, "Lonely Bull" by the Tijuana Brass played on the radio. I was just too miserable to move or even talk. I felt frozen.

It had been a year and a half since I'd seen them, and now here were Dorothy and Ruth and Catherine, and they seemed almost like strangers to me. I felt crummy, so I doubt I looked too good.

I was with them for a few hours, two or three days in a row. I remember we played Monopoly and my folks took me out to eat, but I couldn't talk about my favorite topics, because I didn't want them getting after me.

56

They had two adjoining rooms at what used to be a Holiday Inn in North Topeka. My father wore suits to work, but when they came to see me, he just wore a regular pair of pants and a shirt. I remember my father telling me that if I wanted to use the bathroom, to use the one in the room where my sisters slept. Even though no one would have been around me, I didn't want to go to the bathroom when I was with them. I'd never felt that way before they gave me the medication. Because of that, I didn't think I could stay out too long.

It seemed like I'd belonged to my family when I was little and my sisters had given me a lot of attention before I went to Menninger's, Dorothy for a while when I was little, and Ruth always with a sixth sense about my type of thinking. But now there was a kind of distance. It was like I didn't know my sisters anymore—except for Ruth.

CHAPTER TEN
Does God Really Exist?

Menninger's would take kids to whatever church their family went to if the kids wanted to attend services. But Menninger's itself was completely devoid of religion of any kind. Mom and Dad were very religious, but Menninger's treated God like God didn't exist.

I wasn't practicing any religion and I felt like I was lost. I was so confused. I didn't know what was true and what wasn't. Had they tried to take me to church, I would have screamed. If they sang a religious song in music class, I'd run out of the room screaming.

I'd started wondering about existence and I'd had this horrible thought: *What if God doesn't exist? There would be no heaven or eternal life or anything...*I wanted to know: What happens to you after you die? Is there anything else? It just terrified me, and I shed a lot of tears over that.

I tried to talk to Dr. Albericht about it, that weekend after Christmas.

"Does God really exist?" I asked him.

I don't know what he said, but he couldn't really give me any answer. Whatever he said was of no comfort to me and I cried.

When I left the therapy hour, my family was outside waiting for me. I remember getting into the car, and as we were driving out from the property, I said to my father, "Dad, how do you know God exists?"

"Faith," my father said. And that's all he could say.

And I thought, *Well, faith is just believing something because somebody said it. Why is that any different than fantasy? Why is that any different than things I think?* I started wondering, *Is*

God just somebody's fantasy? I assumed there had to be a God, because we were here, and somebody had to create us.

Then I started having thoughts I didn't ask for about hating God. I was very frightened by them. One time we were on our way to the YWCA to swim and we stopped at a red light where there were two churches on one corner. Thoughts about hating God flashed into my mind. I guess for anybody who was as confused as I was then, a natural feeling would be that they might be angry at God.

I couldn't bear the idea of actually saying the words, "I hate God."

But then I thought, *Well, unless I love God, he isn't going to love me. God won't have a thing to do with me!*

But when I shared this with my therapist, his reaction was just: "So what?"

• • •

There are many things in Catholicism that were quite disturbing to me: holy cards with a picture of a saint or an image of a martyr being tortured on one side and a prayer on the other, and those pictures of Jesus. The crucifix was a terrible instrument of torture, one of the worst things you could do to somebody. Here Jesus was in so much pain, and they never painted tears on his face.

I thought, *How was it for him to hurt so bad and not be allowed to cry?*

Then I thought, *He probably did shed tears when those things happened, but the artist simply left them off. Maybe he thought Jesus would look more heroic if he was not crying.*

When my parents came down, I didn't really want to spend the night with them because I thought they'd make me go to church on Sunday morning. Catholics see crucifixes and the other Catholic imagery so much that they probably don't even think about it. I didn't know how I'd deal with those religious artifacts; maybe being around all those crucifixes and pictures again would set me off. If somebody had tried to take me into a church, I probably would have been so disruptive they would have had to take me right out again.

• • •

1963 was such a sad time. I thought being at this hospital and around these doctors should have done something for me. But every day I swallowed a new dose of hopelessness and fear before I went to the dining room for breakfast. And then I'd be shivering with anxiety half an hour later. I felt as if I had no future, like I was just getting sicker and sicker. And I didn't know what it was. I thought my problem was the fact that I felt anxious much of the time, and that I got upset really easily and couldn't snap out of it, and that noise was too much for me. I wasn't making noises anymore, but still sometimes I'd feel funny in some part of my body and I'd have to keep it moving, like I had an itch that just wouldn't go away. But I'd never known anybody else who jerked or grinned like I did—or who was anxious a lot or who got upset so easily or who was bothered by noise. And because I'd never known anyone who was like that, I couldn't really understand what the problem was. And I thought there wasn't anything anybody could do about it and I just had to live with it.

Nothing went smoothly. If I could get into a situation and not wind up crying and screaming—that's what I called smooth. I was so nervous that the least bit of excitement made my mind race out of control.

What's going to become of me later on? I wondered.

I had no idea what my future was going to bring. Nobody could tell me why I felt like I did; nobody could tell me why I was such a mess. They wanted me to tell them why; they told me I had the answers. And I just racked my brains.

CHAPTER ELEVEN

Metaphors and Subconscious Anger

They had treatment team meetings every six weeks. Everybody who worked with you would get together and talk, but you were not allowed to go to any of the meetings. Everybody knew everything about you, but you never knew what was going on. Their opinions affected what kind of a life you had. They could decide you were "doing poorly" and restrict you. I saw other kids get privileges and then lose privileges. They could do whatever they wanted with you, and there was no way you could stop them. That year I was restricted from public places twice without warning. When I got criticized again and again and again, I kept wondering when I would do something one too many times and wind up being restricted again.

They would twist things I said and talk about "metaphors." I didn't like washing my hair because I thought it was a nuisance. I had dandruff and they decided I needed Selsun shampoos every week. But the person who washed my hair had to put on rubber gloves, because that Selsun stuff wasn't good for your skin. I thought, *If you can't get it on your hands, what in the world is it going to do to my hair?* I'd always complained about my hair, because I didn't like when it got tangled or if it hung in my face. I complained because I didn't like the texture of my hair with that Selsun stuff. It was only years later when I read my records that I saw what they wrote. They'd decided that when I complained, I was really thinking about my pubic hair, rather than the hair on my head.

• • •

I knew I wasn't getting any better, and I didn't know how I would. But I had been told that Menninger's doctors had special training, so I figured Dr. Albericht knew what he was talking about.

He tried to tell me I was subconsciously angry at my parents. He said it and said it and said it. And he finally convinced me it was true. He told me I had to dig up my past and find the answers there. He had this idea that I had all these feelings bottled up and that if I could get the feelings out, my troubles would go away.

I often felt like I was just going to blow up and the people on the unit kept saying, "Control yourself! Control yourself!"

And now here was my therapist telling me I had subconscious anger and that I was holding it inside and I had to get that anger out.

I couldn't understand it, because I could've won an Oscar for the way I acted out—but he wanted me to act crazier than I was already acting.

One day I said, "If I acted as crazy as you want me to, they'd restrict me to my room."

And he said, "Well, if that's the price you have to pay, that's the price you have to pay."

It seemed so strange to be getting conflicting orders. I knew Dr. Albericht wasn't about to take responsibility for what might happen if I did what he thought I should do...it was only a job for him.

He kept telling me and telling me that I was subconsciously angry at my parents, so I started to blame my parents for all my problems.

But if Dr. Albericht could just have been around me and my parents when I had lived at home! I was very frustrated in my relationship with my parents and I often got angry. Consciously and very overtly. I often yelled at them, and I did a lot of complaining. In fact, Dad used to criticize me about my "beefing and belly-aching." I just couldn't see any "subconscious" anger at all. I wasn't angry at my parents now—they couldn't bother me when they were in Omaha. Now I had other people making me mad. I was angry at the staff, at the way they treated me, not at my parents.

· · ·

It was Menninger's twenty-four hours a day, seven days a week. There was nothing else. I had no contact with anybody outside the hospital except my family. They came about five times that year: Easter, summer, Labor Day, Thanksgiving, and Christmas. But when Mom and Dad came down, it was like taking a test in school or playing a piano recital—I knew I'd catch hell if I played the song wrong. Sometimes Mom and Dad would praise me, but always at the same time I was told about my faults. They criticized the way I walked. They criticized my jerking, my tone of voice, my posture. And their ways of expressing it were very obvious: They told me I embarrassed them. I knew I just wasn't what they wanted, that I still just didn't fit.

I couldn't stop thinking about things inside myself and I couldn't think of anything to say that was acceptable. At the slightest bit of excitement, my mind would start to race and there would be something I felt like I just had to do again and again.

I thought I'd gotten so bad I didn't know if I could ever handle leaving Menninger's. I felt like I had just fallen apart, like I was sicker than ever, and I didn't know where it was going to lead.

How am I going to get better if nobody knows what to do with me? I thought. *What's wrong with me? These people don't know how to help me. I'm hopeless.* I thought maybe something inside of me was degenerative and I was just getting sicker and sicker. I was around the best doctors in the world, supposedly, but I was getting worse. I didn't dare voice that fear, though, because I was in a mental hospital. I had to prove my sanity to them, lest I spend my life in a state hospital.

•   •   •

It seemed to me that Richard kept his spark until that spring. At first, he started to seem less friendly. Then he was really mad in his room a few times. And then he became very crabby and aggressive—kind of hostile.

I wasn't aware of him being on meds until the summer of '63. I remember him coming back from a visit in a really bad mood and I saw them giving him Stellazine. During that summer, he started yelling "Out of it!" at me. The others did it too, but when Richard would say it, I just couldn't stand it.

"Out of it, Moran!" he would yell at me. He shouted it in such a gruff voice, almost like a dog, and the sound would really bother me.

•   •   •

Since Thorazine makes you sunburn easily, they switched me to Stellazine in the summer. But just like Thorazine, Stellazine made me feel miserable and I refused to go swimming even though I'd liked it before.

That summer was suspenseful for Arthur. He was almost eleven and he knew he was going somewhere but not where. There were two places being considered for him; one was Devereux School near Philadelphia. He was in the dark for a long time, and it was so hard for him that the stress made him have many severe grand mal seizures at night. The anticipation went on all summer, and I remember Arthur begging the doctor whenever he saw her for some real news about when he would leave and where he would be going. He finally left in late August, but I don't know where he went.

That August there was a certain window—it was on one end of a building at camp, the room where they kept linens. I called it the "little window" and I used baby talk when I said the words. To me it was the building's private part.

Dr. Thomas called it "crazy talk" and she tossed up the idea of me being taken back to the unit and kept there instead of at camp, just as Mom kept saying she could take me back on the train if I didn't stop making noises.

I didn't enjoy camp much. I was very keyed up and had no way to calm down. But I didn't want to go back to the unit.

And in the end, they never did send me back.

• • •

I was taking the medication until February 1964. I didn't complain about it for a long time because I trusted that the doctors knew what they were doing. To me, medicine was supposed to make sick people get well. And it seemed to me that the medication was the only real treatment I was getting; all the other "help" was just nagging and punishment and having things I wanted kept away from me. Other kids took medication, and they weren't acting as if they were anxious. I thought it was my illness that was causing my anxiety.

But finally I began to wonder about the pills Dr. Thomas had prescribed for me, and I started to complain that they made me feel tired. I wanted to stop taking them.

It was a real relief when, after sixteen months, they let me stop.

Once I was taken off the Stellazine and the Ritalin, things changed. People stopped telling me to "Snap out of it!" I felt more comfortable, I was a lot less anxious, and I could tolerate going to school again.

I felt so much better that I started thinking that someday every-thing would work out.

They took Richard off Stellazine, too, and he went back to being the same sweet kid he'd been before.

CHAPTER TWELVE

Whitney Hall

They started saying I was "making progress."

In the younger kids' group, they treated everybody about the same and you never went any place alone. But in the older kids' group, if you behaved well enough, you got privileges, like going shopping with no staff supervision. They were talking about moving me to the older kids' unit. I didn't think I was ready to move in with the older kids, but at least I knew there was an opportunity that they might let me go places unaccompanied sometimes.

So about five or six weeks after I stopped taking the medication, on a Thursday afternoon, I was moved over to Whitney Hall, the older girls' group.

• • •

That year there were a lot of monster movies on TV: giant cater-pillars and bugs and scorpions. I couldn't compete with the TV. They wanted me to just be invisible so they could watch their fantasies—and not have to hear about mine. Also, my room was right next to the living room. This was frustrating because I was a captive audience to whatever was on TV. During the week, you had to be in your room at ten. But sometimes on the weekends they'd have a mystery movie on late at night and I'd never know when a lady was going to scream. If people were yelling on TV, I couldn't get away from it. And I knew that if a sudden noise woke me up, I'd feel upset, so I just didn't go to bed until later and I was always cranky on Saturday and Sunday mornings.

Weekends especially could be so long. I did not enjoy school and waited for the weekend, then wished for something to do on the weekend that I liked doing. The other girls were into movies and sports. But I went crazy because there was nothing for me to do except the things they said weren't right for me.

Also, there was only one childcare worker in Whitney Hall who gave me the kind of attention Belle and Jill Perry had, but she had to leave not long after I moved because she had health problems.

I didn't fit in with the girls on the older kids' unit. They wanted me to learn how to curl my hair. But I was all thumbs and it was very frustrating. My body was almost thirteen years old, but I still felt like a little girl. I wasn't ready to be a teenager.

They might have felt around me the way I'd felt in Children's Corner around the younger kids who couldn't talk, like they'd been demoted to a lower caste. I think I just embarrassed them. I talked too loudly and I jerked my head. One time I was eating chocolate pudding at the table and the fact that it was brown reminded me of poo and it made me laugh. And that pudding just exploded out of my face—*PHHHH!*—all over the table. They were furious. I figured they thought I was a brat.

They started getting on me about my behavior much more than on the younger kids' unit. And they had a network: If you weren't allowed to do something or talk about something, they made sure everyone knew about it. The childcare workers would try to get the other girls to confront you about it. So now it wasn't just the childcare workers chewing me out, the other girls did it too. Everybody was trying to straighten me out. I could see that all the girls hated being at Menninger's. They vented their frustration by scolding me, or they would correct my behavior as a way to get privileges from staff.

They were constantly on me about my tone of voice, about the ways I needed to keep jerking some part of my body, about the look on my face.

Sometimes they'd ask, "What are you grinning about?"

Because the feelings inside were so strong, I couldn't even think about whether I was smiling—or frowning or laughing or looking this way or that way.

Sometimes in exasperation I would say, "Why don't you just operate on my face and make it look like you want it to? Get off my back!"

They'd demand that I behave myself, but then they picked on me so much that they brought out the worst in me. How can anybody act their best if people are keeping them on edge?

They might as well have said breathing was not okay for me. They "breathed" in the pleasure they got from feeling connected with other people. But I didn't—I couldn't—feel that. I had no feeling of belonging, no sense of even existing as a person—nothing positive at all in my life—if I didn't think about objects like they were people. Without my pretend friends (it was church buildings then), life would have been in black and white, with no joy or meaning. But they tried to squelch my speech about that. That was my treatment mode: Don't let Barbara talk about those things.

• • •

One day the girls were getting ready to go out to spend their allowance. That was one thing the group did that I enjoyed, and I was looking forward to going with them. I guess I got a little cranky.

"That's it, Barbara!" the childcare worker said. "You're not going."

This woman had grown up in the country.

"You can't behave like that," she said, "and expect to be accepted. Your behavior is so bad. Barbara, I used to go to barn dances when I was your age, and at a barn dance, people accept nearly everything. But not you, Barbara, not what you do. There are some things people just won't tolerate."

Even in a place where there were no rules, where people could really be themselves—even in a place like that—Barbara Moran wouldn't be allowed.

Dr. Horowitz was the group doctor for the older girls. Sometimes he would say, "She's clinging to her illness."

Once he said, "She doesn't want to be helped."

The pressure to conform made me feel like a reject. It was like I had been banished from society and I would be held hostage until I changed into somebody else—someone I could never be.

For years, Dr. Albericht had been telling me about unconscious anger over some wrong in my life that he imagined, but he ignored the real wrongs I howled about in his office. In Whitney Hall they never gave much thought to my upsets except as a behavior problem. They didn't think about what might have been "bottled up" inside of me.

I also had little common sense and I sometimes said stupid things. Dr. Horowitz told me he wanted me to have speech therapy. I had no problem with speech; I could speak clearly. He wanted me to have speech therapy because my voice was too loud and it annoyed people. It was acting lessons, not speech therapy, they offered me: Act calm, even when you want to scream. I wonder how they would have felt if they could have heard a tape, not of what I said every day, but of everything I heard them say to me. Maybe they were the ones who needed speech therapy.

CHAPTER THIRTEEN
The Older Girls

In the older girls' unit, there were eight girls including me. The capacity was for nine girls, but they had eight.

Denise was going to public school and getting ready to leave at the end of the school year, and Francine was going to public school too.

I didn't think anything was wrong with Sharon, but that maybe they'd put her at Menninger's just so they didn't have to fool with her. There was a divorce and remarriage in her family.

Rita, who had just turned fourteen, had been rebellious and promiscuous with boys. Twila may have been promiscuous too. I remember hearing her say she loved to go to bed, and I guessed she meant having sex. Rita, Sharon, and Twila became like sisters.

Teresa was fifteen, but I think she wished she could be grown up; she wore make-up. She'd come to Menninger's a couple months before I moved to Whitney Hall with a lot of anxiety and depression. Teresa would get very upset sometimes—her life was pretty stormy—and for the first year or so, she just stayed on the unit and didn't even go to school. About a year before, they'd hospitalized her in Knoxville, Tennessee, where she'd had shock treatments every other day—one day insulin, the next day electric shock. She didn't say how long they did that, but she told me that, when she finally went home, she'd forgotten everything. She'd known how to play the piano, but after the shock treatments, all she'd learned was gone.

And then there was Anne. When I moved to Whitney Hall, Anne didn't have any furniture in her room, just a mattress. She would get really violent and they had to keep her in her room with one childcare worker there just to watch. She'd cut herself and I guess they thought that if she got her hands on somebody else when she was really wild, she would have hurt them. Sometimes after dark you'd hear her panic. "I'm scared! I'm scared!" she'd scream, and they'd have to hold her down. They would dope her up with medication, but it didn't do much good. She'd been at Devereux in Pennsylvania for a while and then in another institution before she came to Menninger's. And she'd spent some time on a psych ward in Chicago. Once she told me that if you got upset on that ward in Chicago, they gave you a shot and sometimes even tied you down with leather restraints.

• • •

In Whitney Hall they didn't do much of what one staff person called "entertaining" me. No hobbies and very little one-on-one interaction were offered. In the younger kids' unit, they frequently took us to parks. I always wished I could spend time outside, but in the older kids' unit they didn't do that. In Whitney Hall, the childcare workers were perfectly happy sitting with the other girls and watching TV. Dad was paying big bucks and I doubt he would have wanted me shoved in the corner and ignored with nothing to do but daydream. If "reality" was as important as they kept saying it was, didn't I need people who kept me involved with the real world?

Though I didn't like living there, it seemed to me that Menninger's was a pleasant place to work, and as far as I knew, everyone liked working there. The staff acted content; it was the kids who did the complaining. No staff person ever said "I'm tired" when arriving at work. None of them acted tired, and it didn't seem that they "lived for their days off." It wasn't shameful to work at Menninger's either. In fact, to be a childcare worker was a cushy job. In Whitney Hall, all the girls cleaned their own rooms and did what regular girls do. There was a three-to-one ratio of girls to workers, and sometimes staff would be on the unit when all the kids were in school. Staff was there merely to chaperone and participate in activities: watching TV or playing games. They were paid to do things parents have to pay to do, like going to a movie or for an ice cream cone. They did have to write childcare note updates on each girl from day to day, but there were only eight or nine in the group.

I knew my parents were paying over a thousand dollars a month, and I knew they'd grown up during World War I and the Depression. They didn't waste anything; they wanted to be responsible with money. Mom and Dad brought me clothes during their visits. I had plenty of beautiful school clothes—more than my sisters, who had to wear uniforms to school. Still, I would have loved to be able to buy things I wanted, like sweatshirts or corduroy Levis or a pair of leather boots like one of the other girls had. But I wasn't able to get permission. At Menninger's they had staff who did all the cleaning, staff who set the table in the dining room, etc. There were odd jobs for the kids to do for pay, but I wasn't motivated enough to ask for one.

• • •

That summer, I started spending overnights with my family. One weekend we had two rooms at the Jayhawk Hotel. The weather was nice Saturday and we drove to Kansas City for the day. All of my sisters had come this time. It was the only time Marty ever came to Topeka.

Sunday it was raining and we were in the rooms. The room on the west side had a really good view of Assumption Church across the street. "Tom" was the name I got for the church. Thomas Fitzgerald was the pastor when the church was built, and I called the church Thomas Fitzgerald the Second. There are always people's names connected to a church being built, so if I learn those names, it's no mystery to me what the cathedral's name is. (The reason I use the word "cathedral" is because my parents' church was a cathedral; archbishop headquarters there. And Grace Episcopal Cathedral is in Topeka.)

My folks were trying to teach me a game, but I kept wanting to go over to the window every chance I got and look out at that church, because I had fantasies about it. I went over to the window one too many times, and they got after me about it.

"Barbara! Please come away from that window now!" Mom would say. "We didn't come down here to visit you so you can sit and stare out a window."

On the unit, sometimes if somebody got after me, I would throw a fit. So when Mom said that, I really felt like screaming. I felt very, very angry. I could have thrown one big tantrum. But I was afraid to do that with my parents, afraid I'd be in big trouble if I misbehaved during a visit. I thought Menninger's was doing me a favor by letting me see my family, and that if I wasn't nice when I was with them, my family might go away and I'd never see them again. I was caught between my need to look at the church and other people's demands.

Inside myself, it felt like: "I gotta!"

But I knew people would tell me: "You can't!"

"I gotta!"

"You can't!"

"But I gotta!!"

"But you can't!"

"I gotta!!!"

"Don't you dare!"

"I've GOT to!"

"Don't you DARE!"

"I'VE GOT TO!"

There was just something about my folks. Dad would get after me because I walked with my head down. He'd get after me about jerking my head or about my facial expression. He would even tell me to hold my fork and knife "right."

Once, when I asked Dad what I should do when I was angry, he said, "Well, Barbara, I think one thing you could do would be to run around the block." I was lucky if they allowed me out the door for a ten-minute walk. And then I had to be right back in. They kept me tied up in an invisible straitjacket.

I was so bitter toward my folks after that visit — because they criticized me for looking out the window too much — that I refused to see them for a long time. In August, Menninger's offered me a visit at home. But I wasn't sure what I'd do if I got angry at home. And what if Mom and Dad got angry too? The other reason I didn't want to go home was because there were crucifixes all over the house and I didn't think I could handle that. So in August of '64, I refused to see my family.

* * *

That summer the staff said I couldn't go to camp to stay with the younger girls. The camp was there, the staff supervision was there, the people knew me and could make me obey and keep me safe. But they didn't let me because I was not in that group anymore. They said they wanted me to care about people. There were several childcare workers in the younger kids' group I was very fond of, but they'd just taken me away from them. I felt cheated.

* * *

All the years I attended school, I'd had a feeling of dread at the beginning of every school day. I thought it was my illness. But in Whitney Hall, I didn't have that feeling — I just felt all alone.

In the older girls' group, there were several girls going to public school, and that year they'd sent Rita to Topeka High for a couple hours a day. She was there for two or three months.

A girl called Roxanne came in September. Roxanne was just a year older than me, but she'd had a baby out of wedlock whom they put up for adoption. Before she'd come to Menninger's, she'd had shock treatments too, in a psych ward in a regular hospital.

Patsy came in October. She had what they called "recurrent boils." Some people carry the staph germ and never completely get rid of it. Patsy probably was as clean as anyone else, but they wanted her to take pHisoHex baths—with someone watching. Patsy didn't want to take a bath with people watching her. Once, they forced her to—like they tried to do with Eliza Doolittle in *My Fair Lady*. But after that, the supervised baths were stopped.

During the summer, Anne had been doing better. She had her furniture and even a record player in her room. In late July and August, she was out of her room and when school started she even spent about six weeks in school. But then she had a difficult time and fell apart again. They moved her to the older boys' residence for a while. I guess they figured it wasn't fair to the other girls in Whitney to have her on the unit.

Before they moved her, I would hear her yelling, and it was pretty disturbing—spooky even. Here I was in the room next to this girl who could get really wild sometimes. I had no way of knowing whether or not my problem would get worse too. I remember wondering, *Is that gonna be me ten years down the road?*

CHAPTER FOURTEEN

Cathedrals

When I first moved to Whitney Hall, for a little while they ignored what I drew and I did have fun drawing some unusual pictures. I drew a picture of Westminster Abbey shitting "£" signs.

At first the staff were in their own little world. Some issues of *National Geographic* showed up on the unit, and when I saw one that had some pictures of English cathedrals, I stayed calm and never said a word about it.

But later they began to act like Thought Police, watching me like hawks so they'd catch me in something, just waiting for a chance to get on me. I had to conform, or else. I would sometimes write about or draw my fantasies, and there were times when the staff would barge into the room.

"Show me what you've been writing!" they would say. Then they would look at or read it and write childcare notes. They didn't take my papers away from me, but I knew they wanted me to stop.

I wanted to buy a travelogue about England that had pictures of cathedrals in it. They said I couldn't. By then they knew I liked cathedrals and they knew a travelogue would have pictures of cathedrals in it. But cathedrals had become so important to me that I couldn't stop thinking about them, and when they denied that to me, it was a major loss. There were days when I thought my head would blow off my neck if I couldn't talk about cathedrals.

Sometimes little unpleasant surprises would come out of the blue. One day, I came home from school and walked in to use the bathroom, just like I ordinarily would, and a childcare worker followed me.

She said, "You're on bathroom supervision. You tell somebody to come with you."

I was thirteen years old and somebody had to go in there and make sure I behaved myself! If I'd been six, I wouldn't've minded. But having to ask somebody to escort you to the bathroom when you're thirteen years old? I didn't care if people saw me naked, but I thought that was really degrading for people to see me use the toilet.

I didn't know exactly why suddenly now they thought I needed bathroom supervision. They said our therapy was confidential: In the therapist's office, you could talk about anything you wanted to, and it did not affect the decisions on the unit. At church one Sunday as a child, I'd had an intrusive thought of Jesus wetting and soiling on the cross because he couldn't get to a bathroom. And in Children's Corner, I'd drawn a picture of Jesus wetting and soiling on the cross. But now I used to like to fantasize about church buildings while using the bathroom. I'd put all the stuff I was drawing and writing in a paper bag and take it with me when I went to see Dr. Albericht. On his office chalkboard, I'd draw a picture of St. Joseph's Church sitting on the toilet, with little wavy lines indicating the smell. I also had a thought about the word "mass" related to elimination, like a "fecal mass." Catholics got the word "mass" from "missa," which means dismissal. And "dismiss" means to "send away," and when you "eliminate," you "send it away"...

I was supervised in the bathroom for months.

I was forbidden to talk about cathedrals, even though they were all I could think about. I didn't understand it then, but now I believe it was the long-term effects of those sixteen months on drugs that had created apathy in me to everything else. I wanted to talk about cathedrals so much it hurt.

"I don't want to hear it!" That's all I ever heard people say—and usually harshly.

I felt enraged about this every day, but there was no way out. I had lost the ability to think about anything acceptable. I wanted cathedral-talk the same as I needed food and water. My bottled-up cathedral-talk robbed me of a lot I could have done otherwise—stuff the people at Menninger's would have approved of. But the forbidden fruit was overwhelming.

• • •

I would pretend I was a cathedral, but I kept that to myself since they wouldn't let me talk about it. Because of my alienation from people, I didn't see beauty in a human image. I wished people could look like cathedrals. And I pretended I had a cathedral shape. The body of the cathedral—the main part from back to front and then from the bottom to almost the top—that was like my torso. The fancy part in the front at the top—that was equivalent to above my shoulders and my head. And the apse—that rounded back end of an oblong cathedral—the apse was my fanny. But in my mind, cathedrals also had arms and legs, so that's how I drew them.

If I didn't pretend to be a cathedral, I felt like an empty shell. But they looked on my wanting to talk about cathedrals as if I wanted to shoot drugs.

Was it such a crime to look at cathedrals as human?

That December, my fourth Christmas away from home, was a really dull month with few bright moments. It snowed, and several of us went for a walk. But after half an hour, I was required to go back inside.

Did they think I'd catch a cold?

Right before Christmas (the snow had mostly melted by then), the Westminster Abbey choir came on the TV to sing carols, and they changed the channel right away because they knew at some point the camera would show a picture of the building.

* * *

Every afternoon, Dr. Horowitz would spend about five minutes talking to each girl, and he'd made the practice of taking us outside to walk. Dr. Horowitz smoked cigars and a lot of people complained about them, so he'd sometimes take this time outside to enjoy his cigar. Whitney Hall had a window ledge large enough to sit on around the corner from the living room. Dr. Horowitz started leaving his cigar on the window ledge when he went in to fetch another girl.

Although I didn't like pipe smoke, I did like the smell of cigars. And as a young teenager, everyone thinks about smoking—at least a little taste.

I was often allowed to go outside in the area between Whitney Hall and the schoolhouse, and that meant that sometimes I was there with Dr. Horowitz's unattended lit cigar.

The staff didn't know about my taking puffs from Dr. Horowitz's cigars, so I never got in trouble.

I really liked playing the stealth rebel and being "one up" on Dr. Horowitz, the person who could say no to my simplest request. It was a delightful way to say, "Kiss my little Irish apse!"

CHAPTER FIFTEEN

My First Visits Home

One day early in 1965 they said, "Well, you're not making any more progress." Dr. Albericht was the one who told me. He just said that at their meeting somebody thought my progress had stopped. He didn't tell me who said it, and he didn't say if everyone agreed.

It seemed so arbitrary. I had no idea what they meant. They didn't explain how they measured progress, and they didn't explain why they thought mine had stopped.

I imagined the doctors telling Mom and Dad, "We've done all we can for Barbara. We can't help her. You might as well put her in the state hospital."

I also imagined that maybe they were thinking, *Boy, wouldn't it be nice to get that stupid girl off the unit and get somebody else in here who's curable, or at least a little bit more cooperative?*

Mom came down by herself to visit me and I was with her during the day on Friday. Dad, Dorothy, and Ruth came down Friday evening and I spent the night with them.

At the time, I was seeing my therapist on Saturday mornings. And I spent the entire therapy hour that Saturday crying, wondering if Menninger's was just going to give up on me, since they didn't think I was making progress. And I thought there was a waiting list at Menninger's and that they'd decided they didn't want to fool with me anymore, that they'd give my bed to someone else.

I could just see Dr. Albericht shaking his head and saying, "Dr. Moran, we've done all we can do. Take your daughter somewhere else."

So, I spent the whole hour crying. I didn't know that, while I was crying in Dr. Albericht's office, Mom and Dad were asking my social worker, Mr. Peale, if they could take me home for a day, and that he was giving them permission.

At first I didn't want to go. I was still afraid I couldn't handle it.

My folks took me to the Truman Library in Independence, Missouri, that afternoon, and as we walked around the library, they were giving me a big sales talk.

I mentioned not wanting to see the crosses at home.

And Mom said, "We can take them down."

After I had a chance to think about it, finally I said, "Okay, let's try it."

So, my parents did take me home, just for Sunday night.

It turned out they didn't have to take the crosses down. They bothered me less than I thought they would.

As a little girl, sometimes I told Mom that I felt lonely when no one else was home. And she used to say, "Well, Barbara, you know the way to have a friend is to be a friend."

Her advice to me when I was depressed was always that thinking of others would bring happiness. And she must have tried to believe that, because she was forced to think of others constantly. But I think she sometimes must have felt used, since she did nearly all the work in our family.

I needed to have someone strong, calm, and gentle to take care of me. But I think Mom needed someone like that too. I was not a very lovable child. And my Mom's discouragement coupled with my sensitivity to pain of any kind made it easy for me to believe I was inferior to the rest of the family. I don't know what went on between the child psychiatrist and Mom before I went to Menninger's, but it did not help us understand or even like each other. There was no one to give Mom the support and TLC she needed. Her only outlet was to think and speak of what I was doing to myself.

Dad had a busy schedule too. At the lab, he was in charge of mature adults who were usually easy to get along with. And I don't think he felt the guilt and despair over me and my odd behavior that Mom did. He never was tempted to blame himself. As a doctor, he had seen enough mentally ill people to be sure there was a physical cause that was just not yet understood. I think Dad believed that by the time I was in my twenties, I'd recover.

I think he tried many times to convince Mom that it was not her fault. But how was he supposed to stop the people who gave Mom dirty looks when I misbehaved in public?

I think she was ashamed of having a little girl who was not like other children. I sensed my mom's discouragement, and that made me feel alone. No doubt she felt alone.

But Dad did have a great sense of humor. I got a kick out of how he'd sometimes mispronounce my name. "Bar-BARE-a," he'd say. I later learned the name "Barbara" actually means foreigner or stranger; it comes from Latin.

Once when I had a visit home and he came back from work and saw me, Dad said, "Hello, stranger." Maybe he said it because I simply wasn't around much anymore.

In May, I had one more visit where half of it was in town and the other half was at home.

Down at the corner drugstore, I bought candy and a postcard. The postcard was a picture of St. Cecilia Cathedral in Omaha, which I called Cee-Cee.

Everyone thought I'd only bought candy at the drugstore, but then Ruth walked in the bedroom and caught me looking at the postcard and grinning and talking to myself about it.

My family put together a report for the social worker about how I acted during the visit, and Dr. Albericht talked to Mr. Peale and he told me what my family had said. Marty had told them I wrote the word "Cecelia" in the sand at a beach where she took me. And there were some comments about the postcard from Dorothy or Ruth.

• • •

Ruth

In the years after Barbie left, life went on in our household, of course. My older brothers and sisters started getting married, and then there were grandchildren. And so when Barbie was inserted back into the family, she was a stranger to us. No one understood what was wrong with Barb, or what to do about it. And her way of interacting became...well, perhaps not stranger, just more of the same—where her objects were much more important to her than people. No one had a clue what was going on.

Early on, Barb was just another kid and the whole family adapted to her peculiarities. But she went away, and when we started seeing each other again as teenagers, it was very hard, because she wasn't expressing herself. Terrible pain emanated from her. The level of intensity was incredible. And there was nothing you could do about it. There was just no soothing her.

• • •

Back at Menninger's, I got so angry. Now that I'd had a taste of my family's world, I knew what I was missing. Life was going on outside and just passing me by. Maybe, just like people in prison, I got stuck in perceiving my family's home as it was the last time I saw it. But David and Ruth and Dorothy—everyone else was growing up. And my life was going nowhere.

Menninger's had a track meet that spring. I wore a cardboard number at the meet, and I got to be outside for several hours. I even won some ribbons. Afterward, I put the ribbons on my bedroom wall surrounding the cardboard number. My room looked cool.

But then I started thinking about my life. I'd been at Menninger's for years. I was older, but at fourteen I still had volatile emotions. I was in many ways more rigid, compulsive, and preoccupied than ever.

I thought, *How I can become interested in people?* And, *Why do people have to be so boring?* And then, *What is so bad about me talking about cathedrals, anyway?*

A few days later, I took all the ribbons and the cardboard number off my wall and tore everything up. Then I cried. I also tore up pictures of my family. I was so jealous of my sisters and brothers. They had a life and I didn't.

• • •

In high school, my brother David was friends with an exchange student from Germany. That year, he had German records and even German cartoon books. Then David had two years of college at Creighton University in Omaha, and when he'd saved up some money, since he knew German well enough, he went to Germany and took some classes at a university. At the university he met Pedro Aguinaldo, and they became good friends. My parents really prized "brains," so when David wanted to bring Pedro home with him in 1963, they were happy to take Pedro in, and he became an honorary Moran. Pedro learned English, went on to study American law at Creighton, and got a job. In August 1965, Pedro married a local woman, and his family came over for the wedding.

My family wasn't able to have me at the same time, because it would just have complicated things. I was just starting to have visits home, and I didn't really fit in. I went home after Pedro's family left—and that's when they told me Ruth was going to Spain. Because of my family's welcome of Pedro, the Aguinaldos said they'd be willing to take one of the girls. Ruth was at the age that she'd try anything, so she decided to spend a year in Spain. I was sad because I'd finally started having visits home and I wanted to be with her. Now she was going to be gone, and I really felt cheated.

Mom and Dad took me out hiking in a forest in Omaha. On the way, we happened to go down a street by a church building I liked. It was being remodeled at the time and it looked just awful. It was like they'd bludgeoned him to death and left him lying there. My feelings were intense. It was like seeing somebody in the street who'd been hit by a car. I had a sick feeling in my stomach. But I didn't dare say anything. I knew that if I'd told Mom and Dad how it bothered me to see the church looking like that, they just would have scolded me. "That's ridiculous, Barbara!" they would have said. "That's nothing to get upset about."

CHAPTER SIXTEEN

Fancy Clothes and Safe Men

The Pope, Paul VI, came to the United States in 1965. I thought he was cool. I started thinking about popes and cardinals and bishops and the kind of clothes they wore. And I had fantasies about those people. I would think about them like I would think about objects. Sometimes I pretended I was the Pope and Menninger's was Vatican City. And since at that time the Beatles had long hair and Sonny and Cher wore bulky vests and bell-bottom pants, I thought I would like to wear a bright cassock on the stage and a huge cross, about three inches long on a chain like the Pope wears.

Because "pope" means "father," Dr. Albericht decided I had a sexual thing about my father.

Nobody at Menninger's but the social worker and Dr. Horowitz had ever met my father. No one at Menninger's ever bothered to ask how I really felt about Dad. No one bothered to ask if I was content to have Mom and Dad for parents. I tolerated my parents in order to get a change of scenery once in a while and to eat the foods I wanted. Life with my parents was an unending power struggle—and they held all the chips. I had no say in the way they or anyone else ran my life; all the decisions were made by others. All I could ever do was beg for favors—which I usually didn't get. I didn't enjoy their company. It was hard to talk to Mom and Dad. They'd been taught to dare not have emotions, and I was always a very emotional person. Mom and Dad never accepted me as I was. And there was nothing about Dad to make me feel romantic. My father criticized me a lot; he was not a comfortable person to be with. When I was born, he was turning forty-seven; and when I was fourteen, Dad was sixty-one. There isn't any way I could've been in love with my Dad; he certainly wasn't sexy.

When I made up stories about anybody, I always molded the person to be what I wanted them to be. It was impossible to imagine anything about people I already knew; reality wouldn't let me. If I'd actually known priests or the Pope, that would have killed any imagining. All those guys in the Catholic Church had taken a vow of chastity, so I considered them "safe." This was in the days when no Catholic sex scandal was ever publicly discussed. I was very naïve about men then.

When I had a thing about the Pope, it was actually the Pope, strutting around in those fancy clothes, not my father.

· · ·

Dr. Horowitz didn't think that boy-girl relationships should be allowed in mental hospitals. But there was an ambivalence about that issue. They would sometimes try to discourage it, but other times the girls and boys got to spend time together. It always seemed to me that, if you put a bunch of teenagers together—unless they're really crazy—the girls are going to like the boys and the boys are going to like the girls. I thought they should be happy that the girls liked boys because I couldn't get interested in them.

I was not attracted to boys. That's what really puzzled me: the fact that the other girls fell in love and I didn't. I couldn't see what they saw in the boys. But I wished I could have, because it was "normal"—everyone falls in love, right?

Rita was crazy about boys. One night she went to a party and came home drunk. And then she tried to run away, but she didn't make it. She was restricted to her room and not allowed to talk to anybody on the unit except staff.

Rita's room was next to the living room and right across the hall from the office—the room they'd put me in to start out with. You had to pass by Rita's bedroom window to get to the living room. And the boys would come down to see us.

Eventually, they painted over the window in that room so Rita couldn't see the boys.

But then later, when one of the girls who had been going to public school and had a boyfriend on the outside, became pregnant, there was no "shame on you" talk at all about this. She did have a lower status and had to be accompanied off grounds. But she was allowed to go anywhere the group went. And once the baby was born and was put up for adoption, she was allowed to be out on the grounds anywhere unaccompanied. In the fall, she went back to public school. Menninger's seemed to be less disturbed by this girl's pregnancy than by my fantasies.

CHAPTER SEVENTEEN

To Get Out of Menninger's

In January 1966, I'd been at Menninger's for four and a half years and there was no sign I'd ever get to leave. Still I thought, *Good things happen to other people, so it's gotta happen to me.* I started begging Dad to take me home. Dad kept saying I couldn't come home because I wasn't able to go to public school. I knew then that I had to do whatever I could to get out of Menninger's.

Menninger's had nothing to offer me. They fed me and put a roof over my head and made sure I went to school and did my homework—and at least that gave Mom and Dad some respite they badly needed. But as far as being able to change me for the better...well, Menninger's idea of changing me was just getting me to act right. I realized that if I was going to find help, it was going to have to be somewhere else.

Everybody got out of Menninger's sooner or later, one way or another.

If you were able to please the staff, that was the way you got out of Menninger's. Then there was a progression. The first step was you went to public school, and after you were getting along there, they moved you in with a family. They referred to the foster families as "boarding homes," but the families worked for Menninger's.

In order to be acceptable, I would have had to give up every-thing that was inside me, so there was nothing left of the real me, whatever that was. But I made up my mind that I would try to please them, even though it would require living a double life. I began to do a lot of pretending and lying and fooling. I started by trying to keep my fantasies to myself; I would try not to talk about them and I would try not to write about them.

The thought of regular school terrified me. But I was desperate to get out of Menninger's and I thought maybe Dad would let me come home if I was in school. So, when the principal of Menninger's school walked through our unit, I asked him if I could go to public school. He said I was "too conspicuous" for public school.

But then Dr. Horowitz and others decided to let me try it.

Dad wanted me to go to Hayden, the Catholic high school in Topeka.

I didn't want to go to a parochial school.

Dr. Horowitz said, "You don't have to go out to school at all."

I wasn't about to say no, because I thought if I didn't go to school, the state hospital might be my future. Hayden was the only choice they gave me, so I said okay.

I think Dr. Horowitz sent me to Hayden because he knew Dad had made a big compromise. Years later in my records, I read Dr. Horowitz's description of my parents as "downcast" when they met. My parents had put me in Menninger's only because there was no Catholic place. As a Jewish man, I believe Dr. Horowitz understood how painful that decision had been for Dad. I think Dad and Dr. Horowitz had a lot in common; he had daughters of his own.

CHAPTER EIGHTEEN

Traffic Lights and Tornados

The weather in spring of 1966 was beautiful: lots of sunshine and very little rain. At Menninger's we generally made a few trips to the basement every year for a tornado watch. Once I'd been taken from the bathtub. But there'd never been any damage in or near Topeka. And that spring, no tornado watch had been issued.

After dinner on the eighth of June, we left Menninger's to go shopping with our allowances, me and some of the girls in Whitney and a childcare worker. On our way to the White Lakes Mall, the clouds were gathering. In the mall, I bought a pair of rubber thongs. I had just gotten my change when they blew the sirens. All the stores closed and put their barriers down as we made our way to the shelter.

After about thirty or forty-five minutes, they blew the sirens to issue the "all clear," and sunny weather continued as soon as the storm was over.

But it was incredible how Topeka could be turned into a pile of junk in half an hour. The older kids at Menninger's volunteered at a distribution center sorting clothing donated for people who needed it. I helped make sandwiches in the kitchen there with donated food, so I got to see it all up close. I saw some smashed apartment houses. Washburn University was hit hard and most of their old buildings destroyed. A huge chunk of metal was missing from the capitol dome. Most of the downtown stores were spared, but the tall building on the southeast corner of Kansas Avenue was unusable even though still standing. All the windows were blown out.

I'm sure many traffic lights—if they were smart—ran for cover when the sirens went off. But on the corner of Seventeenth and Washburn, I saw several dead traffic lights who hadn't been able to decide whether to take cover or stay where they were. One signal had had his legs anchored to the pole by the wind; his body was badly twisted.

We were all allowed to call our parents, but instead of calling, I wrote a letter telling them everything, describing the tornado and how Topeka was ruined. I was wishing they would take me home, but I knew they had their minds made up and they would not. Once before I wrote a letter begging Dad to take me home. Mr. Peale didn't even send the letter; he gave it back to me.

CHAPTER NINETEEN

Jealousy

My sister Dorothy studied Spanish in college that year (she went to Creighton like David, Pedro, and Ruth), and she went over in June to stay with the Aguinaldos. When she and Ruth came home the end of July, they brought one of Pedro's sisters back to Omaha with them. I never knew she was coming until I came home for a visit and she was already there.

Dosa was fourteen, a few months younger than me. She was really nice and didn't know about me, which made that summer a little more pleasant. People who didn't know much about me usually were more open-minded; if they knew too much, they tried to run my life.

Her name was really Rosa, but when we tried to roll our r's, it came out "Dosa," and everybody started calling her that.

I got to stay home that summer until school started. In August, Pedro and his wife took Dosa sightseeing, and I went with them. That was a very busy month: Go! Go! Go! Fun! Fun! Fun!

Sometimes Ruth, Dorothy, Dosa, and I were all out with Pedro, and they spoke Spanish. I didn't understand a word. I could always learn what they were saying, of course, but much of the subject matter wasn't relevant. I was into talking, not listening, after all.

Lucy Johnson, daughter of President Johnson, got married that summer at the National Shrine of the Immaculate Conception in Washington, D.C. I had a thing about that church, and they had a picture of it in a news magazine. I took the magazine upstairs and kept it in the bedside table in the drawer for the whole month. It was one of the happiest months I've had.

Ruth told me about the first couple of months over there in Spain before she got to know the language. She said she'd been scared before she went to Spain. And then she asked me if I was scared to be going out to school.

I was petrified. I had been doing high school work when I moved into the older kids' unit, but schoolwork was always hard for me. I couldn't get interested and got frustrated easily. I dreaded starting school. I imagined myself alone in the halls surrounded by strangers, crying like a baby and not being able to stop.

But I couldn't admit to Ruth that I was scared, because I worried that, if I actually thought about it and talked about it, I would get more scared, and then I'd get upset, and then I might not be able to go to school at all.

But not being able to talk about that just made things more difficult. I had a lot of feelings to talk about then, but of course in my family feelings were not talked about.

• • •

Dosa adjusted because she knew Ruth so well, but she was homesick and sometimes felt very sad. It was a long time before she learned English and we weren't really able to communicate, but it was just so neat having somebody else there.

The household had to be bilingual, because I knew English and no Spanish; Dosa knew Spanish and no English. Ruth and Dorothy spent a lot of time talking in Spanish so Dosa could understand. At other times, everyone spoke English.

Dosa must have been really brave. One night at the table she got weepy and Mom put her arms around her and, even though Mom didn't know any Spanish, she said, "Is it too much English, or too little *español*?"

When Dosa heard Mom say *español*, she smiled.

You could tell Mom reached her. Dosa knew she cared.

That summer, my tics began to go away. When I realized I was changing, I tried super hard to get them to stop. And for the most part, they did stay away, although still today in my sixties I can have some minor tics when I'm under a lot of pressure, since they're a way to relieve tension.

I was thrilled that Dosa was there. She was another teenager around at home. I felt like I had a friend.

But back at Menninger's, Dr. Albericht said, "Don't you think that girl's there to replace you?" He even asked me, "Aren't you jealous of her?"

• • •

Mrs. Moran

When we took Barbara back to Topeka (by that time Barbara was coming home for longer periods — usually two weeks), Dosa and Ruth went along. I think maybe Barb felt a little bad that Dosa was living at her home and she wasn't, but whenever Barbara would be back home during that year when Dosa was with us, there was a lot of contact between Pedro and Dosa and our family — all of us; it added a dimension to life. At first Dosa didn't speak any English, but when she was starting to learn, I remember that on the trip back, one of the things Ruth did was to sing little ditties with her like, "Things go better with Coca-Cola; things go better with Coke …" Ruth said it was easier to learn to sing in a language than it is to speak it first. And Ruth would have her put a pencil in her mouth to hold her tongue down, because she was determined Dosa was going to learn how to speak English without any accent. And she did — before she went back to Spain, she spoke perfectly.

CHAPTER TWENTY

Hayden High School

In the fall, I attended Hayden High School two hours a day, the second and third periods, two days a week. I took American history and English. Everybody'd get up and say Hail Marys in the beginning of the class and kids went to Mass once a month. Most of the teachers were nuns and they were still wearing those old outfits: all in black to the ankles with this thing around their heads that looked like blinders and the veil on top of that. When I saw in the student handbook that paddling was a punishment Hayden used, that disturbed me.

I tried to make a good impression: I wore nylons—even put on cologne—and tried to be a lady. I never said a word or caused any trouble, but I felt like an outsider in that classroom, like I was from another planet.

They didn't have school uniforms at Hayden; everybody wore regular clothes. I wore sweaters or blazer jackets. I hated it when I had to wear certain clothes just because they were in style. I wanted to wear longer skirts—a little below the knee. It was the childcare worker at Menninger's who got me to wear my skirts above the knee, and I always felt my bottom end was inadequately covered. But wearing my skirts shorter than I would have liked was at least something that I could "do." I had to endure a lot of anxiety and I couldn't get my face to look right, but I could wear the clothes everybody else was wearing.

It was hard for me to concentrate. American history was so boring that one hour seemed like a whole day. I used to do my history homework in front of the TV to stop the thoughts I didn't

97

ask for that would interfere with me doing my work. I always needed to have a radio or something on. I did my best: I outlined the chapters and answered all the "section survey" questions, even though you only had to do one of them, because I wanted the extra credit so I wouldn't flunk the class.

A few days after school started, the English teacher wanted someone to read "The Bells" by Edgar Allen Poe and I volunteered, because I wanted to be a star. I had no idea what she was looking for. I read the poem as if I were a sports announcer, like a 33 rpm record played at 78. Later on, the teacher played us a recording of the poem read dramatically. That's what she was looking for.

But I just kept telling myself, "Once you go to regular school, they'll let you out of Menninger's."

• • •

In the afternoons, I was back at Menninger's for school. For a while Anne had lost weight, but then she started eating everything in sight and she was having trouble controlling her weight and she got fat. I think it was because of her medication. She had started gagging herself. During their lunch break, the teachers would come to units and visit and chat with us. I don't know why Anne complained she felt nauseated when my teacher came on the unit, but every time Miss Woolf walked through, Anne had to go and vomit.

We had some encyclopedias on the unit and Anne read the article about mental illness. It said schizophrenia was character-ized by rapid mental deterioration. After she read that, she began to say her brain was deteriorating and she was going to die. The staff continually tried to tell her that her brain was not deterio-rating, but they never got anywhere. I'd read that article, and I thought it was ridiculous too.

When Anne found out her family's finances couldn't keep her at Menninger's any longer, she announced to the group one day that she would have to leave. And she began to fall apart. Maybe it was the fact that she was leaving Menninger's and she knew there wouldn't be any help for her anywhere else that made her feel like she was going to die.

* * *

In the summer, before I started at Hayden, Menninger's attitude about my freedom had changed. They started letting me go places unaccompanied. I could walk over to a Dairy Queen, and sometimes they let me go downtown. They also had decided in the staff meeting that they were going to make me go to the football games. No one asked me if I was interested; they just took me. In September, Hayden played the first game at a city school near Menninger's. The stands were packed, so I sat on the top of a parked car and the childcare worker who took me stayed at a distance. After that, I went to the games by choice. You were outside and you could move around, and the atmosphere was kind of fun.

A boy came around and started talking to me. He had red hair and freckles and he was fat. He attended Hayden too, and he told me his name was Paul Jackson. He said he'd been in some sort of psychiatric facility in Washington State for a couple years and had just come back. He also told me he'd gotten high on morning glory seeds, and he talked about two boys he said were his "drinking buddies." He wasn't even old enough to drink.

I just needed a chance to be with somebody, so I decided football games were okay.

Hayden won the game. Paul Jackson got my phone number and he called me in the morning. This total stranger tried to tell me he couldn't stop thinking about me.

It was a bit exciting to meet a boy, but then I didn't know what to do with him. I didn't think I could trust him, but I tried to go through the motions of "acting normal."

Menninger's said I could go to the next game and on a date to the school dance, if they got to meet Paul. He came over to Menninger's to visit me one afternoon about a week later, and we sat outside and talked.

One of the other girls was out there with her boyfriend, who also lived at Menninger's. She was crying hysterically. I was thinking that if any boy ever made me cry like that, I'd never want to see him again.

Paul called me on a regular basis after that, and he wound up taking me out a few times. His parents would drop us off and pick us up, so I never had to be alone with him. I considered the boy/girl thing to be social, and that's all I wanted. But he got infatuated with me and wanted to give me a Maltese cross with a surfer on it to wear as a going-steady symbol. The staff intervened.

I did not respond to boys the way another girl would. Paul wanted somebody to fall in love with him, and he thought he was in love with me. I didn't have any feelings like that at all. He was a total stranger; it was really very awkward. Once I said to him, "How could I love you? I don't even know you."

• • •

Topeka was a real mess and for months they were talking about the tornado, which was one of the biggest on record. It took a while to rebuild. But by the end of the summer, the city was functioning and life was pretty much back to normal. The buses were running and Washburn had set up trailers for classes while they worked on the buildings. I didn't see much more than that. One Sunday, a radio preacher said, "God sent the tornado to tell us He is here." No one needed to hear garbage like that after such a devastating event. Many people lost their homes and businesses.

I didn't imagine that God cared enough to do much of anything, for me anyway. I thought God must approve of all the misery everyone had engineered into my life—the Menninger's staff and my parents. It really hurt to want help so bad—and for my parents to pay so much trying to get it for me—only to hear a lot of empty promises, and then realize I needed to hide who I really was. My life was not my own. I felt like, for me, life's bicycle was only a stationary one: I could pedal all day and not move an inch.

• • •

In October, after I got to know some people at Hayden, one girl asked, "Are you going to join pep club?"

I decided to join so I could feel like one of the crowd. People in the pep club wore the outfit and sat together at the games. The staff at Menninger's must have been surprised, but they got me the uniform. There wasn't any place you could buy the skirt; it had to be made. Fortunately, there was a childcare worker who was good at sewing, and she made a really good blue skirt with box pleats. And they got me the pep club sweater: blue and white with a big "H" on it. I liked the color blue, and when everyone was wearing the uniform on Fridays, it was good to feel I belonged; it was a way to be like other girls. And I think the people at Menninger's were happy to see me going to school events. But I was trying to prove my sanity by faking what they wanted me to be. And I was full of anxiety of being discovered—caught at being myself.

• • •

When I was home in early November, I asked Dad, "After I go to regular school all day, for a semester, could I come home?"

I thought maybe in the spring I'd be at Hayden all day.

And he said, "I want you to graduate from Hayden."

That was devastating. I felt betrayed. I got the feeling my folks were saying, "We don't care if you go to a regular school; we just don't want you home."

Dad had told me I couldn't come home because I hadn't been able to go to school. And now finally I was going to school and it was like in *The Wizard of Oz* when Dorothy got the broomstick, then was told to go away and come back tomorrow. It seemed as though every time I managed to obey the rules, they changed them—the requirements just went up and up and up. I was crushed. I was fifteen, and it would be a long time before I'd graduate.

But I kept thinking, *Maybe I'll change his mind down the road.*

CHAPTER TWENTY-ONE

Some Kind of Incentive

One day I was outside the school waiting for my ride back to Menninger's. Someone came outside carrying broken glass to throw away. Some part of a stage set had been accidentally pushed through a window. Because I thought of the building as alive, this upset me and I couldn't stop thinking about it.

There was no sense of being welcome in anyone's presence at Hayden. Paul Jackson kept up his thing about being in love with me, but I knew it wasn't real. And I didn't want a guy who was such a rebel. I had to invent a reason to like going to school there. I needed some kind of incentive so I could feel close to someone.

I'd seen the school building before I'd started school, because it was right on the main drag. I'd just never paid much attention to it. But now I started having a thing for the Hayden High School building. Freshmen and sophomores went to the old school downtown, but juniors and seniors went to the new school, the one I was going to, which they called Hayden West. West was, to me, the building's last name.

Hayden West was oblong with three floors. Everyone went in and out on the north end. But I imagined the other end, the south end, being the front and I imagined the face being on that side.

It didn't make any difference whether I was inside or outside of it. If I considered the building to be a person, that made it more pleasant to be there; it was like being close to a friend. If I could have drawn that building, I think I probably would have drawn it with a smile. But I'd already decided I should stop putting things on paper, anything somebody would see. I had to keep it all to myself, buried in my head.

On Fridays, I looked normal: I was wearing that pep club sweater, just like most of the other girls. But nobody realized the sweater also had a special significance to me. Inside the big "H," in the middle, was the word "Hayden." And of course, Hayden was the name I had given to the schoolhouse.

Menninger's had childcare workers whom they referred to as "floaters," who took kids out to several schools. That first semester they took me over at 9:30 and picked me up at 11:30, so I never really got a chance to talk to Hayden.

But later on, when I was attending school all day and walking home, before I went back to Menninger's, I'd walk around to the south side of the building and say goodbye. I doubted I could be seen back there, and no one ever caught me there at the little niche at the south end. I wanted to be there looking at Hayden West's face. It was very satisfying to stand out there and talk out loud, like it was a conversation. Buildings don't talk, of course, but they can listen, and I just sort of thought I knew what it wanted to say.

I knew the schoolhouse had been completed in December just a few years before. So, I asked the schoolhouse what he wanted for Christmas.

"I'll bet you want some toy cars and trucks," I said, "and Creepy Crawlers...I'll bet you want the Twister game...Well, don't count on anything, Hayden—you've been bad all year!"

* * *

Mrs. Moran
By that time, one of her big fantasies or personifications of things was buildings, and she would get these strange looks on her face—and a little bit, I won't say out of control, but enough so that it was a worry that she might get run over or something, 'cause she might be staring at the building and not paying attention to traffic.

She would cry on the way back to Menninger's. When she was going to high school at the first school she went to, in order to give her the maximum time at home, when she'd stay over the weekend, I'd get up at the crack of dawn on Monday morning and drive her back to Topeka in time to get there for a nine o'clock class in the morning. And those were very difficult times because she cried quite a bit on the way back. It was just Barb and I for the three-hour drive. Well, she was very unhappy to go back; she wanted to stay at home, I'm sure...

• • •

More babies were being born into our family every year. My brother John and his wife had several children, as did my sister Marty and her husband. But when I was home for a visit, I was able to survive because that house was big enough that I could go where I couldn't hear them.

But that Christmas my parents got a puppy. Dorothy had a friend whose dog had puppies, and Dad let her bring one home. Fluff was a white spitz-collie mix. When I first saw him, I thought he was so cute. But on Christmas Eve, he was outside in our fenced-in yard, and he was trying to get out. He kept going this way and that way like he was just desperate. He wasn't crying or howling or anything, but he looked so helpless out there. And that image of helplessness was like my own helplessness. It was depressing and it made me cry. Going to a regular school, even for two hours a day, was such a strain. And because of the stress of school, my noise sensitivity had gotten worse. I felt small and vulnerable like the puppy, like I'd spent my whole life behind a fence saying, "Let me out! Let me out! Let me out!"

On Christmas Eve I didn't eat dinner. Instead, I went upstairs and cried. Ruth came up and spent time with me, but the rest of the family just went on, business as usual, like I wasn't there.

• • •

In January 1967, when I came back from the holidays, I wondered where Rita was. In the fall, she'd started going all day to public school, but she had sex with somebody, and in November they'd discovered she'd gotten pregnant. They took her out of school.

Over the holidays, she'd been in the hospital. The childcare worker told me she'd lost the baby. I didn't know if she meant she had miscarried or that they'd done an abortion on her. They sent her home from the hospital a little bit sooner than they'd planned because she was throwing things at people.

One night—I remember Rita had just gotten her hair done—she managed to slip out of the building after dinner, and somebody must have met her nearby. They even had the FBI looking for her, but they never found her. We heard later that somebody in Texas took Rita in, and that eventually she called her family and begged them to take her home and they did.

Around that time, Anne's parents took her out of Menninger's. I think she might have gone to a state hospital.

Paul got into a fight in the school parking lot that year and got into trouble other ways too. But I guess he also wanted to make himself more socially acceptable, like I did, so he tried to do all the things normal people do. He took me out a few times more, but then maybe the feelings wore off. He never mistreated me, but he was not the best choice for a companion. I think the only reason I went anywhere with him is because no one else ever asked me out. But we were never more than two strangers. I wasn't comfortable with him, and he wasn't comfortable with me.

• • •

The second semester that year, I was at the Catholic school for half days, three hours, and had my afternoon classes at Menninger's.

Every first-hour class at Hayden attended Mass once a month, since the teensy chapel was big enough for only one class group at a time. I was so desperate to look normal that I decided to see if I could handle going to the services. While I'd been at Menninger's they had changed from the Latin Mass and I hadn't been to a Mass in English before, so that first one was pretty novel. But when I walked out of that room, I was soaking wet with sweat. You would have thought the temperature in there had been a hundred degrees.

Every time I went to Mass, I'd be irritable all day. At Menninger's, one childcare worker told me she knew going to Mass was sheer hell for me. I never really knew how she knew. I never tried to get out of going, though, because I just wanted to fit in.

I went to the basketball games too. But basketball is so fast and so wild and the acoustics were awful and of course everyone was yelling. I'd get keyed up and I just couldn't handle it. And somebody from Menninger's had to start going along to keep an eye on me. One time I felt I had to make this motion over and over again: nodding my head up and down. And they took me home before halftime.

In the spring, Menninger's started talking about moving me into a "family care home" or "boarding home," as they sometimes referred to them. This just meant placing a client with a family. But with going to school, I felt like I had to jump through hoops just to survive and that if I couldn't do what other people did, I might cross some invisible line that would make disasters come. They said I had "regressed" a little bit, and the move was postponed.

When summer came, the Catholic school had no summer program, and I took a psychology class at Topeka High School. On the first day, the teacher said how strict he was going to be and how he had a temper. He told us he would really make us work hard, that he was going to make sure we got frustrated. His name was Thad Tira and he said, "If you can pass my class, you can make it in a college class." I guess he just wanted to make sure people would toe the line with him. But once you got to know Mr. Tira, he was pretty entertaining. And psychology was something my brain could respond to. It had nothing to do with an interest in people. I was looking for an explanation why my life sucked. The people at Menninger's told me I was mentally ill, and I was looking for answers just to make sense out of life.

Timothy Reston was in Mr. Tira's psychology class with me. He was still at Menninger's too. He was small and slender with dark hair, a little awkward. And, just like me, sometimes Timothy's train of thought would lead to something funny and he'd laugh—usually at the wrong time. He also talked in monotone. With that odd-sounding voice, I imagine he'd heard his share of cruel comments disguised as counseling from both staff and the other boys. At parties he would dance with me, but it felt empty, as if he were just trying to prove his sanity by being like other people. I thought he tried to put up with me because none of the other girls was interested.

Generally, I would feel happier and less anxious during the summer, when there was a lot of sunshine and I could be outside more. But that summer I was just as anxious as during the school year. Besides attending Topeka High for the first time, I was also the emperor's wife in the play *The Emperor's New Clothes* at Menninger's. In September 1966, Dosa's brother and her sister-in-law had had a baby, and now when I went home, it made so much noise that I just couldn't be around them. But by August, Dosa spoke English very well and we had a good time taking long walks together. Once Dosa and I decided to walk over to the Goodrich Dairy for malts. Dad gave us a dollar. Malts were a quarter then. We got four of them; she drank two and I drank two! I had a thing about the high school building in Omaha too. Nobody knew. But Dosa and I walked by it at least once or twice every day.

Sometimes the whole family would drive down to Victory Lake near Freemont, just outside Omaha. We'd take a picnic lunch and spend the day there. Hardly anybody knew about it, so it was almost like it was our own property. The water was so clear you could see right through it. It was the best of two worlds: fresh clean water and a beach—and no little kids around, so it was very peaceful.

Dosa got so attached to my family, she didn't want to leave. But at the end of August, when her brother and his family moved to Philadelphia, she went with them and from there flew home. Once she got home, she wrote to us and said she was glad to see her own family.

• • •

In the fall, we studied the prologue of *The Canterbury Tales*, and we were to write a poem describing people going somewhere. I decided to write about a group of girls going to a basketball game, and I wrote brief descriptions of several girls who were in the class with me. One of the girls was very cute with short, very well-groomed auburn hair. She always looked really good, but her pep club uniform was a hand-me-down. And that's what I wrote about—just her uniform. I didn't even bother to write that she was a really attractive person. The girl saw my notes. No doubt they cut her to the quick. I was used to hearing rude, hurtful remarks about my appearance and behavior at Menninger's. I had little empathy and I hadn't learned tact. After all these years, the memory of my insensitivity to her feelings still makes me feel ashamed.

I was very much aware that I didn't fit in. Hayden was a private school; people had to have money in order to go there, and it seemed like everybody was so sophisticated that I was way behind them. I don't remember anyone actually calling me names, but some kids made fun of me and said things that were unkind. Other kids made funny sounds when I was around. I don't remember anyone actually calling me names, but sometimes there's just a way a person acts that says, "I don't want you around me ..."

In my English class, though, a boy who sat behind me would say words like, "Beeeea-ver." I thought that was funny! He wasn't making fun of my behavior; that was just what boys would do with girls.

Still I had butterflies in my stomach—like when you're going to the dentist—most of the time. Sometimes I would get very anxious and upset. Often, I would call the childcare workers on the unit back at Menninger's. And during my lunch hour, I went to talk to the counselor at school. He was caring and I got sympathy from him. It continued to be very difficult for me to go to school at Hayden—but I remained terrified of what would happen if everything fell apart.

CHAPTER TWENTY-TWO

You've Chosen to Be Mentally Ill

For a long time, Dr. Albericht hadn't put much pressure on me. It seemed he was more permissive and open-minded the first few years I knew him. I thought I liked him. But when I was going to the Catholic school, he started shaming me.

When I would talk to him about my experiences at Hayden and about the way the other kids treated me, he would tell me it was my own fault. "Your behavior's all wrong," he said. "I can't tell you how, but it's all wrong."

He also said the other kids had a right to tease me because I made them anxious.

"They have to put up with your behavior, Barbara," he'd say. "If you'd act better, they'd treat you right."

And then he'd tell me I was "copping out." I was supposed to figure it all out myself.

The fact that going to regular school made *me* anxious wasn't important.

One day he said, "Barbara, people make choices in life. I think you've chosen to be mentally ill."

CHAPTER TWENTY-THREE

Riccardo

At Menninger's, there were a lot of simple problems with communications. So in the summer, they'd started having hour-long joint meetings with the staff and the girls, once a week on Wednesday in the conference room. You wrote down on a list what you wanted to talk about, and everything was discussed openly. Anything anybody wanted to say, they could say it. This straightened out conflicts, eased the tension on the unit, and improved everybody's attitude.

At one of those meetings, in September, they announced that somebody had given a record player to Menninger's, a console.

I wasn't sure I wanted that thing in the living room, because I didn't know how I'd react to it, wondering mostly how I'd feel, if I'd get intrusive thoughts about music when it wasn't on. But when they brought it into the living room the next day, my first thought was that it didn't even look like a phonograph; it looked like a chest of drawers, like it couldn't produce music. That definitely helped.

One day they were working on the phonograph when I came home from school. And that night I dreamed of a record player with surgical bandages taped on it. And then another night I dreamed I was polishing the phonograph all over. After I had those dreams, the phrase "record player" made the word "Riccardo" pop up in my mind and I started calling the record player Riccardo.

One Friday night, everyone else went to see *The Taming of the Shrew*. I didn't want to go. The childcare worker who stayed with me wanted me to clean the living room, even though it wasn't my job. I polished Riccardo all over like in my dream. And I was able to get away with it, because everyone was unaware of how much I liked him.

To me Riccardo was a trophy, a catch, a way to feel like I'd scored. I'd pulled a fast one and they never knew. Polishing Riccardo all over that Friday night got me hooked. I wanted more of him. I polished him again Sunday afternoon.

But on Sunday, everyone was there and they saw me.

When I'd come back from my home visit in August, right before school started, there was a new girl on the unit. She was six feet tall, as big as a man, and she was quite an intimidating person. The name Goliath came to mind when I first got a glimpse of her. Another girl came that fall too, and those two got to be real buddies.

"Moran!" the big girl said, when she saw me with Riccardo. "You're making an ass of yourself."

"What if we talked to the refrigerator, Moran?" said the other girl.

I said, "It's fine with me!"

Another time I put some 45s on Riccardo and I said, "You'd better work or we'll call the repairman." I don't think my talk about the repairman bothered him; he probably thought it was funny.

Being with Riccardo was thrilling and I felt high, euphoric.

But the girls thought it was just horrible.

"Moran! You're talking to a record player! What's wrong with you?"

But I was proud of myself: I was a bad girl. I was worn out trying to be nice. I hated everything about my life except Riccardo.

It made Riccardo mad to see how the other girls treated me.

At Christmastime, Riccardo completely broke down. He was intact—you wouldn't have known he was busted—he just stopped working.

And the next day, that tall girl dragged him down to the stairwell.

I had a feeling of horror, like my best friend was in a dungeon. I didn't dare go down there to see him, but I kept trying to find excuses to pass by him on the way to somewhere else.

• • •

At home, that little puppy my folks had gotten the Christmas before had grown up. Now he would stand by the terrace door when Dorothy and Ruth were home and he would bark and bark and bark—every day—on and on and on. He'd also bark at the neighbors who were trying to get in and out of their house. I kept hoping somebody would come over and complain. Mom and Dad were generally quite submissive to anybody on the outside. For instance, they never questioned anything Menninger's told them. So I thought that if a bunch of people came over and complained about that dog...

But no one ever did.

Later on when I went home for visits, Mom finally realized babies bothered me and she went out of her way to keep them away from me. But she never understood the dog bothered me as much as the babies.

Everybody would complain about my behavior and my voice, but the dog could just roar all day and that was all right. For me, that dog's barking was just overwhelming, like having somebody hit me—it was that much of a strain.

Mom kept talking about how he'd protect us and how he wouldn't let anything happen to us. It didn't matter if the dog drove me crazy.

• • •

In January 1968, when I came back to Menninger's after the holidays, Dr. Horowitz told me I could visit Riccardo in the stairwell any time I wanted to.

I think Dr. Horowitz assumed people would regress a little when they got ready to leave the hospital, that the stress of the big change could make things a little bit harder for people briefly, but that once they were out and the transition took place, they would bounce back and do better.

I used to write Dr. Horowitz letters when I wanted to appeal to him for privileges. I wrote him letters because if I did too much talking, he said I was nagging him, but when I wrote him the letters, he read them. Maybe I made more sense on paper than talking, and the ink on the paper didn't grate on his nerves like my tension-filled voice. I think he began to see the "real girl" in me trying to get out and be noticed. He was such an open-minded doctor, he became a hero to me.

Riccardo and I "came out of the closet," and because of Dr. Horowitz, the staff were understanding. They let me talk to Riccardo, and I was never punished for having a thing about him. But the other kids still thought I was acting stupid.

One day I came back from school and Riccardo was gone. They'd given him to a thrift shop in Topeka. I missed him, but I was happy to think of him being somewhere a family might find him and take him to their home where he could be happy for years and years. I loved him so much, that's what I had to believe would happen to him.

• • •

They wanted to put me in a foster family that had a two-year-old and a baby on the way. I'd talked and I'd talked about my little nieces and nephews bothering me when I went home for visits. Finally, I was allowed to turn down that foster home.

There were two more foster families available. One was a widow, but they didn't want me to move in with her, they said, because they wanted me to be with two parents. I don't know if I could've fit in there with the widow anyway; I never found out if she had a dog or if her house was a quiet place. The other foster family had a couple of college students. One of the boys was in college in Oklahoma and one went to Washburn. Neither one of them was married and I thought there wouldn't be kids in that family for a long time.

When I meet most people, I usually have no opinion about them because they're strangers. But when I met the Harrisons early that February, it did not feel right to be with them. I thought my foster mother was a very intimidating person—just her physical presence, before she even said anything. I did not feel at home in their house and I had no desire to live with them. But I felt moving to a foster home was my only way out of Menninger's. So I agreed.

• • •

Mrs. Moran
Menninger's didn't call it a "foster home," but it was supposedly a step out to bring people back home. They said they took great care in trying to get just the right person, but how little they knew about Barb...They told us the background of these people. He'd been in the service and they had friends throughout the country that they often visited and would probably do quite a little traveling and they would take Barbara with them. Well, they didn't know up from down about Barbara if they thought that was going to be beneficial and she could cope with that—she couldn't cope with that at all.

• • •

Dr. Horowitz realized that if I had to change before I got a life, I'd never get one. That was his way of looking at me all along, but

I think it was only years later that he told me his decisions in my favor were based on the fact that he wasn't going to put my life on hold until I changed.

In mid-March, when Hayden's basketball team lost a game against Topeka, I snuck down to see the Topeka High schoolhouse and I beat on the schoolhouse wall with a belt. I was just fooling around; a little belt couldn't hurt a stone building. But at Hayden the next day, one of the girls asked me about it and I panicked, thinking I'd be in big trouble. The fact that the girl saw me made me realize I was right out in public and anybody could have seen me. I thought somebody would snitch to Menninger's and I'd get in trouble. So I went and confessed to Dr. Horowitz and to the staff that I had done something stupid, because I figured if I told them first, I wouldn't wind up getting put on restriction. I think Dr. Horowitz had a sense of fairness and learned from his mistakes, if no one else at Menninger's ever did. He had an interest in me just like a father. He talked to me on his own time and I don't think he ever charged for it. So, since I was getting ready to move to the boarding home, Dr. Horowitz cut me slack.

• • •

A man named Teddy Hesse had replaced the principal of Menninger's school who'd thought I was too conspicuous for regular school. That spring, probably around April, the end of my junior year, I was talking to Teddy Hesse and, who knows, maybe I had the look of someone who's been pushed too far. I didn't beg him or anything, I just asked him about going to Topeka High.

He said, "Okay, Barbara, if you want to go to Topeka, I'll enroll you."

When Teddy Hesse told me I could go to Topeka High, I felt like Santa Claus had just dropped a gift in my lap. Even today I don't know why he let me have what I wanted. It's still surprising to me, because my complaints had usually been ignored or criticized.

Finally! I thought. *No more Hail Marys.*

• • •

The day I moved to the foster home, it was hard to say goodbye, but I didn't think anybody could *not* want to leave a mental hospital, because that would really be "sick." We took my stuff out of my room and put it in the car. Everybody said goodbye to me. But I didn't say anything, even though Menninger's had been my whole world for a number of years. I just got in the car and left. I was afraid they would tell me I was clinging to the hospital.

Me with my siblings in 1951. In front, left to right, are Ruth, Marty holding me, and Dorothy. In the back are David, John, and Catherine.

Me at age five, 1956.

Me with Ruth and Dorothy, 1956.

My First Communion, May 1960, in Omaha, Nebraska.

On the day of my brother John's wedding in 1959: From left to right are my dad, Clarence; me; Catherine; my sister-in-law Sandy; John; Ruth; my mom, Miriam; David, Marty, and Dorothy.

Me on my eighth birthday in 1959.

My family's first visit to see me at Menninger's, December 1962.

Me (left) with Ruth, Dorothy, and Catherine in the parking lot of the Topeka Holiday Inn during a family visit to Menninger's in 1963.

Me at age twenty-six at Lake Perry, outside of Topeka, 1977.

Reggie and Annie dressed in plaid and my apartment decked out for Christmas, 1994. (Rooney's off to the right.)

Rooney, dressed up for Christmas, 2016.

I love traffic lights. The ones from the 1950s are the real live ones, but they're an endangered species these days.

I traveled to Denver to meet Ernie, Union Pacific Steam Engine 844, my favorite choo-choo.

To me, Ernie is like a big, friendly animal.

Here's a close-up of my embroidered Ernie tribute vest.

In 2018, I got together with all my sisters in Omaha: (left to right) Catherine, Dorothy, Ruth, and Marty.

PART THREE
Menninger's: The Foster Home

My Washburn University yearbook picture, 1969.

CHAPTER TWENTY-FOUR

Life with the Harrisons

In May 1968, when I moved into the foster home, I was like an outpatient, still seeing the social worker and therapist.

My foster mother, Constance, told me, "Whatever you do in your room, that's your business."

No more Thought Police. I could draw and write anything I wanted.

And the Harrisons had no pets, so that was nice.

But there were plenty of negatives. First, the house was so tiny that if there was anybody making noise anywhere in the house, there was nowhere you could go. Even in my room, it was just like if a TV is too loud and somebody turns the picture off: blank screen, sound still on. Then, there were no buses in that part of Topeka, and it was a long way to anywhere I wanted to go. And there were no sidewalks in their neighborhood. Whenever it rained, the mud was ankle-deep. Also, the Harrisons knew a family with a two-year-old, and they visited occasionally. So sometimes there was a baby crying in the house.

I complained. Once.

"That's ridiculous!" Constance said.

When Constance was growing up, she told me, her family kept a razor strap hanging in the kitchen so they could use it to whip the children. My Dad had a razor strap too—to sharpen his razor with. He never hit anybody, not even his sons. Constance never actually threatened me, but sometimes she'd talk about what she'd do with me if I were hers. Constance was about ten inches taller than me and large-boned. Next to her, I felt like a little girl.

She was full of syrupy-sweet phony-politeness when I first met her. I never felt as though I could trust her. I never felt respected or appreciated or welcome. It was as if by having me in her house, Constance was doing a penance.

While I was at Menninger's, I'd been allowed to go out alone and I sometimes came home late. But I never had use of a key. I was let in and out like a dog or a cat. Now all of a sudden, I had to get used to things people usually learned earlier. They gave me keys, but no one helped me rehearse.

No "What do we do when we're the last one home?"

No "Now, Barbara, remember: When you get home, lock the door and then turn off the outside light ..."

Or "Make sure you lock the door if you're the last one to leave the house ..."

Once when I came back, I was thinking about turning off the light and I forgot to lock the door. And I got a lecture about how someone could have just walked in and I could have ended up "having a little colored baby."

I felt as if Constance expected me to make mistakes. Whenever I goofed up, she said, just like the people at the hospital, that I was "in my own little world." I knew that meant she didn't think she could count on me to be responsible.

Bruce Harrison had been in the Air Force for twenty-three years. They talked about what they'd done when they lived in Italy and Virginia, about the things they did now at their church, about the department store where Constance worked—she'd been working in department stores since she was a teenager—and about Bruce's job with the state helping veterans find jobs. But if I talked about Menninger's, they said I was boring everybody, that I was interrupting or dominating the conversation.

One day we'd gone to a restaurant with another couple, and

they were talking about some boy who ran away from home. It was interesting and I asked a question.

Constance said, "It's none of your business."

When some of their friends came to visit, they could see I was blocked out of conversations. They could tell I wasn't always treated right, but they didn't know what to say. I didn't know how they felt until years later when they became my friends.

For the first year, I tried to stand up to Constance. Once I told her that talking to her was like talking to a brick wall.

Bruce was friendly, though. Sometimes, just to be funny, he would mispronounce my name the same way my father did: "Bar-BARE-a." He didn't criticize me the way Constance did; he often just let me be myself when his wife wasn't around. I didn't have to censor all my favorite things out of my talk. But that first year, he had part-time jobs in addition to his regular state job and he often wasn't home until after 9 p.m.

The older son who went to Washburn was shy and didn't talk much. But when the younger son was home from college in the summers, he had a great sense of humor too, like his father, and was a fun person to be with.

But it was Constance who was around most often. Back at Menninger's, they had to include me because I was part of a group, and there were some staff who showed me affection. Now I had only one way I could make myself feel loved and happy—and that was if I pretended objects were like people, the way I had since early childhood. And so at my foster home, I felt more alone than before.

• • •

By this time, Timothy Reston was in a boarding home too. I was still at Menninger's when Timothy started visiting the boarding home. After he had his first visits, he was describing the foster mother and father and their kids. He wound up in the family with the babies, but he seemed to like the children. He told me that the boy, who was two years old then, made a lot of jokes about dirty pants. He said things like, "Stinky in your pants," and Timothy thought that was funny.

In June, when Ruth came down to visit for a weekend, Constance served her tacos and let Ruth drive her car, and I thought Constance liked having her there.

Ruth and I cleaned my room and lined the drawers with newspaper, and Ruth took me to a record store that sold hard-to-find records.

Summer school had just started: two days and then the weekend. On Saturday night, Timothy called and wanted to go to a movie. He'd graduated from Topeka High and was going to start college in the fall. I wanted Ruth to meet Timothy, so I thought the three of us could go to a movie together. But when I asked, Ruth said no. I guess, since she'd gone out of her way to come to Topeka and she wasn't going to be there long, she wanted to be with me and not somebody else.

But I didn't understand that then, so I said, "Okay, why don't you just stay here, and Timothy and I will go out?" When Ruth was in Spain, Dorothy and Catherine would leave me home with Mom and Dad when they had dates. So I figured I could leave Ruth with the Harrisons. I didn't know there was anything wrong with it. I thought Constance had showed Ruth real hospitality, but maybe it felt as fake to Ruth as it did to me when I had my first visits to the Harrisons' house. But both Ruth and Constance said no, so I got back on the phone with Timothy and told him I was busy that evening.

Constance told me months later that Ruth couldn't come back because Constance had felt like tearing her hair out that weekend

Ruth visited. I thought that was strange, because the Harrisons had lots of company, sometimes two or even three families to lunch on Sundays. But maybe she didn't like having another family member there watching her—somebody in my family who had more power than I did.

· · ·

I took a biology class at Topeka High that summer. They were working on the floor in the gym, putting in a new floor, because the other one was just shot. The gym and the classrooms were all under one roof, so I could walk down and peep in. And then I had trouble thinking about anything else. When summer school was over, I went home for a month in August. Ruth and her boyfriend took me to an ice cream parlor. I'd told Ruth I thought the school building was in pain and it was driving me crazy. So, when they asked me what flavor I wanted, I ordered the maple malt.

Ruth understood that I'd ordered the maple malt because I knew the gym floor would be made of maple wood.

"Does it taste like a gym floor?" That's what Ruth asked me.

· · ·

Ruth

I remember how she would go on and on and on about the reconstruction of the gym floor, but her ability to describe what was really going on was very limited. All this pain and all this emotion supposedly generated by construction on this building—it left us...we didn't know what to do. I always tried to read into it: "She must be telling me something about something else. She must be trying to say something about life." But there was this wall of intensity coming at me. We couldn't really converse back and forth, and it was very hard to get to the bottom of anything. I felt helpless in the face of it.

· · ·

Since public education is free, I was on a more level playing field at Topeka High. At Hayden, everyone looked too good, too sophisticated, and I could not compete. I found the kids at Topeka High to be real people, and I fit in better.

Still, the tension from living day to day was so great, like static on the phone drowning out the voices. Some people at school would talk to me, but I had no real friends. Because of my nervous and loud behavior, most people acted as if I were a nuisance. I could only imagine what regular girls said when they talked about boys on the phone. Topeka High put the wrong number for me in their phone directory, so if anybody wanted to call me, they couldn't. And I was wondering if anybody ever tried. When I got their numbers, I called. I called all kinds of numbers trying to start friendships, but I couldn't get anywhere with anybody.

There was one girl in my art class, though, who I was chummy with. I was even at her house once. But Constance never offered to bring her over to our house, and a cab would have eaten up too much of my allowance even for one trip.

CHAPTER TWENTY-FIVE

Troy

I imagined that the schoolhouse loved me and believed in me. The Topeka High School sports teams were called the Trojans, and they often referred to the school as the Halls of Troy. So, I called the building Troy. I considered the tower its head, and I spent as much time as possible talking to it. I'd sit on Troy's front porch after school and any other time I could get there.

I told the building things I would have talked to people about. I even talked to the school about social issues, like injustice and the way they treated Black people and what was really happening in Vietnam. And I imagined the school telling me to work hard on my lessons and that it was proud of me.

Sometimes, when I was keyed up and silly, I feared the school would think I was laughing at its troubles. But they were doing that remodeling project and I would say, "I really do feel sorry for you, Troy."

I'm sure nearly everyone noticed me at one time or another. A few of the kids made fun of me.

• • •

My senior year, Timothy and I were still going to school dances and places together quite a bit. But he wanted a real companion and I was too preoccupied, too apathetic toward people, so there was always a lot of tension. My behavior sometimes got on his nerves, and I was so anxious that being around other people was nerve-wracking. Both Timothy and I were trying to be good, trying to live up to expectations the hospital had put on us, trying to refute the negative feedback—to get people to believe in us. We never really enjoyed being together, but it was something we both felt like we were supposed to do, because we knew that's what other people did.

When I was still at Menninger's, I had started riding one way on the bus from Topeka to Omaha, and then Mom and Dad would take me back. Even though someone at Menninger's would drop me off at the bus station, it was still a big deal for me. I was desperate for autonomy. I just wanted to get out and be myself, and being alone at the bus station gave me a little bit of peace and quiet sometimes.

When Christmas came, I was going to take the bus home to Omaha. At Menninger's, the staff and patients never exchanged Christmas gifts, so I did not expect to get presents from my foster family. I had carefully selected presents for everyone who would be under the Moran family roof that year: Mom, Dad, Dorothy, Ruth, Catherine, and David. But I wasn't even going to be at the foster home for Christmas and no one had told me the rules would be different in the boarding home, that I was allowed to buy presents for the foster family.

Just as I was getting ready to leave for Omaha, out of the blue Constance gave me a beautiful white sweater.

I tried to save face by handing her a couple of dollars and saying, "Merry Christmas."

But Mom told me I hadn't done it "graciously." She sent them a poinsettia with my name on the card. "I just knew you wouldn't buy them anything," she said.

CHAPTER TWENTY-SIX

Fantasy Will Set You Free

By 1969, I was seeing Dr. Albericht only twice a week. During the summer, I'd seen him three times a week, but in the fall because of the school schedule it was reduced to two times, so I didn't have to miss much school. And it was twice a week after that. When I first moved into the foster home, I remember telling him that somebody did care about me. I was thinking about my foster father and the activity director and some other people at Menninger's who had been friendly with me even when they didn't have to be.

But Dr. Albericht said, "Those are paid relationships."

I didn't know what Menninger's would do if I said I couldn't stay with the Harrisons. I lived with the fear that if the Harrisons decided they didn't want me, I might be put in the state hospital for life. I felt stuck. After that first year, I was always saying I was sorry.

Dr. Albericht had started to dress and act like a hippie. He'd had New Age ideas long before the rest of the world did, but now he grew out his hair, started listening to psychedelic music, and bought bell-bottom pants (though he still had to wear a jacket at Menninger's). He even put up a poster on his wall that said "God grows his own"—whatever that means.

At first I thought all that was cool, but I was still young and too naïve to realize he was acting very childishly: The man was thirty-eight that year and he didn't want to get old, so he tried to be a teenager. Years later, I heard that one day some staff member opened a closet and found him standing on his head, meditating.

He used to listen to the Steppenwolf record with "Magic Carpet Ride." He seemed like a hypocrite to me, though, because that song said, "Fantasy will set you free." Yet he hated my fantasies.

CHAPTER TWENTY-SEVEN

Ramada Inn

In early June, just after I moved in, the Harrisons' oldest son had gotten a job as an assistant manager at a department store. He had been working in the store where his mother worked. Because he was making more money as an assistant manager, he was able to get married not long after he started the new job. And in the summer of 1969, they had a little girl. The son was attending classes in Topeka and still working at the department store. His wife worked full time. The grandchild didn't live with us, but now, instead of being gone some evenings each week at church activities, Grandma Constance babysat. And when Grandma wasn't babysitting, it was because the young family was there for the evening. So instead of having the house to myself sometimes, now the baby was there almost every day.

When I graduated from Topeka High on my eighteenth birthday, May 29, the Harrisons didn't go. Constance was having some medical problems. First, they did a minor procedure, and then they had to do major surgery and she was off work for several months to recover from the operation. But Mom, Dad, and Ruth came down. At the outdoor ceremony, it rained at just the right time, so we didn't have to sit there and listen to them call out names one by one for hours and hours.

Losing the Topeka High building was like what a child goes through when a parent he loves no longer has custody or even visitation rights. I cried over Troy for months.

The thought that I'd have to try to find a job terrified me, but I started looking even before I'd finished school. At the same time,

I wasn't sure I could handle working. I didn't feel ready for the adult world, so I took another typing class at Topeka High, just to be around that building again. But they did more remodeling that summer—the biology unit, the locker rooms, and the pool in the gym—and that really bothered me.

I applied for jobs at a lot of places, but people would say, "Don't call us; we'll call you," like they didn't feel comfortable with me.

I went to the employment agency to try to get help. The counselor would give me a paper saying, "Go to such-and-such a place," and I'd get there and they'd say, "Oh, we filled that job last week" or "We hired somebody a long time ago."

I didn't know if they were telling the truth, and that was very frustrating. It took me two months to find a job.

My first day at work was July 31, 1969. The coffee shop at the Ramada Inn was no place for a person like me.

The job was just routine stuff: picking up the dishes and taking them back to the kitchen and then setting up the table for the next customer. But there was too much noise and confusion and it seemed to me that, whenever there was a crying baby in the room, the tables right next to that baby were always the ones with the dirty dishes on them. The hours of 4 p.m. to midnight were horrible, and the cab ride home ate up two hours' pay. I'd always had poor coordination and was accident-prone, and restaurant dishes are heavy, slippery, and breakable, and I dropped a lot of them. They tolerated this for a long time because at least I showed up for work and did the job. But I frequently felt depressed. I used to tell people I never had more than seven bad days a week.

Actually, no one enjoyed working at the coffee shop. There was no safe place to hang your coat and keep your things, and it seemed as if everyone was looked upon by the hotel as a potential criminal. So people generally didn't stay more than a few months.

I had three different supervisors while I was there.

My father insisted on my going to college, and Ruth thought maybe I'd like it too. So while I worked in the restaurant, I also started attending some classes at Washburn University. I worked six hours a day, thirty hours a week, and I went to college seven hours.

Even though there were a couple of buildings at Washburn that I thought of as alive, they weren't good enough—not like the high school building. And I felt too young to be in college; the environment at Washburn seemed too grown-up for me. It was worse than any school I'd been to.

I did complete all three of the classes I took. But that year was so stressful—between Washburn University and the job at the Ramada Inn and the baby at the foster home—that I began to have a lot of upsets. And I actually got physically sick. It seemed something was always going wrong on Friday. Tension would build up during the week, and nearly every Friday I'd get a cold or I'd be vomiting or I'd have diarrhea.

After her operation, Constance wasn't allowed to drive for six weeks. The military hospital where she went was very slow getting the results of her tests back, and she'd lost twenty pounds worrying whether she had cancer.

One day I thought I would walk to the nearest bus stop, about ten blocks away, then get off the bus and see the schoolhouse first before I went to the Ramada Inn.

But Constance knew me: She'd picked me up at school enough times that she'd seen me talking to the building. She knew I had cried since I'd finished high school because I wasn't able to be around the building anymore.

She said, "I can drive now. And I'm not letting you go near that school."

It was too early to go to work, so I asked to be dropped off at the Super D drugstore. I thought I could still go see the high school and then go to work.

I don't know how long she would have waited if I'd gone into the store. But I didn't go in the store—I tried to go right to the school.

Constance followed me.

"Get back in this car, Barbara," she said. "I told you you're not going to see that school building anymore."

And after I got in, she said, "Tomorrow I'm taking you straight to work."

I cried and protested, but she said she was going to put a stop to it.

"Barbara! Listen to yourself," she said. "You're reacting as if that school was a man!"

But the next time we saw Mr. Peale, the social worker, he told Constance not to stop me from going near the school. He said if I wanted to see it, I could. But he made it clear what he thought of me.

"If you want to talk to buildings, Barbara," he said, "that's your business. I have no intentions of stopping you. But I want to tell you that I think your behavior is bizarre and crazy. It's like… well, it's like going to the bathroom in the street."

• • •

The Ramada had two restaurants: the coffee shop, where I worked, and the Le Flambeau Club, which had both a bar and a restaurant, along with carpets and plush chairs.

There was a guy named Mark who worked in the Le Flambeau Club, and one day he asked me out.

Mark was a gentleman. He played gospel music on his car stereo. He took me roller skating and then we got something to eat.

He told me Jesus was his life. I think he would have made a good husband for someone, but I had nothing to bring to him. I was so stunted that I had no feelings left except to cry, to scream, to sulk, and to pretend to talk to the objects I thought of as human. I had no empathy, no connectedness. All around I could see other people who seemed to be able to connect, but I didn't even know the language of humanness.

CHAPTER TWENTY-EIGHT

It Chose Me

When I saw Dr. Albericht after being with Mark, I started crying and I couldn't stop. Mark had been really nice to me, but I was just so abnormal and so out of synch with people, I didn't know what to do with this guy. I knew I just couldn't be part of a relationship or friendship like that. I was unable to think about people. The thoughts just wouldn't come. It was like trying to get a glass of milk from an empty carton. Here this guy was being really nice to me, but I was so dysfunctional, I couldn't relate to guys the way ordinary girls did, and he was kind of wasting his time with me. I guess I just felt bad because I couldn't be like other girls.

I didn't scream about Mark, but I often felt like screaming when there was too much noise. During that year, there was just too much noise in too many places. I had such extreme rage. I would call my social worker or my therapist on the phone and scream about my life. I had no idea why I needed to cry and scream so much. No one in my family screamed. No one at work screamed on the phone to anyone. My social worker, therapist, foster parents—none of them ever felt the need to scream. The DJs on the radio didn't scream. Mark never screamed; in fact, he seemed calm and content.

I knew life wasn't perfect for other people. They got mad; they complained. But, for one thing, noise to them was only sound. And it seemed to me they felt good much of the time.

I hated everyone for leaving me behind. I knew they must not feel like I did because they never acted like I did. I blew up in people's faces a lot that year. No one blew up like that in my face, not even my foster mother.

Dr. Albericht would suggest I try this or that.

And when I said "I can't"—because I really couldn't—Dr. Albericht would tell me it was because I didn't want to.

It didn't matter what I said or how strongly I wished for my life to go right, Dr. Albericht would say my "phantom self," my unconscious, was choosing to be mentally ill.

And there is no mercy for someone others believe has chosen failure.

But I didn't choose failure; it chose me.

• • •

We had Thanksgiving dinner twice that year because all the Morans were home. Mom and Dad had a professional portrait taken before the second Thanksgiving dinner on Saturday. And they were thrilled. It was a rare occasion: All seven of us were at home. That was a luxury for them. But after the picture, I disappeared. I just needed a quiet place, so I stayed upstairs shortening some pants I'd bought. Everybody in my family wanted me to be something I couldn't be. If they didn't like me as I was, I decided I didn't want to be with people like that.

• • •

I didn't have any fantasies in the restaurant until around Christmastime. In December, I had a thought I didn't ask for: A restaurant table was telling me it liked me. I wanted out of there fast. The next day, I vomited at home and called in sick. And then I was off work for Christmas vacation and not due back until New Year's Eve. I hoped the craziness would go away when I went home.

But when I came back after New Year's Eve, I couldn't resist: I started talking to the tables at the Ramada. I made up names for all of them and I couldn't stop thinking about them. It didn't make my job any easier. It just made me look stupid.

All of 1970 was stormy for me. Life was difficult every place I went. In my foster home, the baby couldn't last more than fifteen minutes without crying—I timed her once. There was no quiet place in that house. The only choice I had was: Do I want the baby at home to upset me, or do I want the customers' babies at work to upset me? I felt trapped, sad, and adrift. Tension built up and I was getting upset more often. And when I got upset, I would usually call my therapist, or maybe the social worker, and scream on the phone.

I started thinking more and more about religion and the Stations of the Cross and those pictures of Jesus with a terribly pained look on his face because they're whipping him. And I began to get thoughts I didn't want about sharp objects. I wasn't afraid I would hurt myself or someone else. Instead, sharp objects, anything I could be cut with, reminded me of stormy emotions, plunging into my stomach, cutting up my soul. Some of this came from Catholic imagery, those pictures of the Virgin Mary with all the swords pointing toward her heart and the ones of martyrs embracing their instruments of torture. Images like that kept intruding on my thoughts. Of course, I never told my therapist because it was just too bizarre. Thoughts like these made me believe I was crazy.

I had no business working in that restaurant. I couldn't handle it there. The Ramada Inn was not the proper place for me, and it wasn't fair to the other Ramada Inn staff for me to act the way I did.

One Sunday in early July, they were having a banquet in the Le Flambeau Club. Late that evening, someone told me they'd changed the furniture for the party. I had to go and peek, like I did when I was five and I wanted to see the book about the locomotives, like I snuck down to see Riccardo. I couldn't stop myself.

The tables had been stacked in the ballroom, upside-down on top of other tables like people hung up by their feet. It upset me so much; it was like they were being tortured.

In my head, I knew the tables were nothing. But after that night, I started having even more upsets. My behavior became disruptive. I got very, very compulsive. I was out of control. And I started having trouble just getting the work done. Before the end of the month, they ran out of patience and let me go.

CHAPTER TWENTY-NINE

After the Social Club

The Mental Health Association had started a social club and I arranged to go one night in July. I'd been fired from my job; my foster parents' grandchild was now one year old and crying nearly every day at the house. And, as happened every year in July, Dr. Albericht, my therapist, and Mr. Peale, my social worker, and Dr. Horowitz, who used to listen when I called or stopped by and cried to him—all the people I thought I could trust—were on vacation. I was at an absolute low and felt abandoned and alone in the world.

I remember getting ready to go to the social club. I put on bell-bottom pants and a dark T-shirt with a regular neck and short sleeves, the kind of thing everyone was wearing then. I guess I hoped to find a friend, but when I got to the club, I felt like I didn't belong there either.

At the end of the evening, a volunteer was taking people home. I knew who he was and that he was authorized to drive people, so I went with them. First, he dropped off a couple of ladies at a nursing home. When they got out, I was the only person left in the car. I thought he would take me to the foster home, but he started driving toward southwest Topeka.

All of a sudden he said, "Take off your clothes. I want to play with you."

I thought he was kidding. But he wasn't.

While we were driving, he undressed me against my will. I tried to escape, but I never made it out of the car. Whenever another car came near, I yelled for help.

And I kept screaming at him: "Please take me home! I want to go home!" I was terrified. I was wondering whether he had a gun in the glove compartment. I didn't know what he was thinking, and I was afraid he wanted to kill me. He seemed sadistic, like a psychopath. I was begging and begging: "Take me home. Please don't do this to me."

He threatened me: "Do you want me to hurt you?"

He acted as if he enjoyed my horror.

He said, "If you don't cooperate, I'll fuck your ass."

He had one hand on my breast and one on the steering wheel. He wanted to feel my crotch. At the hospital, I'd heard of a girl being raped and murdered in Topeka and her body thrown in the bushes somewhere in the country. Now, looking out at the stars, I wondered if I'd live to see another day.

He stopped the car and put his penis in my mouth.

Finally, I got control of myself and I said, "Can't we compromise?"

After that, he lost interest and then took me home.

I ran into the house screaming, "I almost got raped!"

Constance put her arms around me and tried to comfort me. I definitely felt like she warmed up to me in a way she wasn't able to do at other times. But at the same time, I had the feeling she also wanted to say, "I told you so," because I had gotten in a car with a stranger.

Menninger's had a social worker who took over if there was an emergency while your social worker was on vacation. When I saw her a day or so afterward, she said, "If you press charges, it would be your word against his."

I was only nineteen; I wasn't a legal adult yet. I would've needed somebody to help me press charges—like a family would press charges if something happened to their daughter. I didn't have any backing, no support. Menninger's just didn't want to get involved. I knew this guy's name and I knew he'd been in the state hospital. Certainly, six psychiatrists and two social workers—from Menninger's and the state hospital—could have helped me press charges and get this guy put away. Maybe he even had a history of abusing women.

But there was no attempt to press charges. I remember thinking: *If I'd been murdered, maybe Menninger's would have said to my folks, "You know, Dr. & Mrs. Moran, you still owe us, because we reserved the bed at the foster home for the whole month."*

When I told Timothy Reston that the guy had molested me—Timothy knew this guy, too—he didn't believe me. I got really angry then, and I yelled at him on the phone.

When Dr. Albericht came back from vacation, he said, "Well, Barbara, you know if you ever do get pregnant, I'd be able to help you get an abortion."

We'd talked before about the girl who was raped and murdered in Topeka, because it was worrying me. Now, when we talked about it again, Dr. Albericht said, "Barbara, let me tell you the way I look at it: If rape is inevitable, just relax and enjoy it!"

CHAPTER THIRTY

Bertram

I wrote Mom a letter and told her what had happened. She told me that when she read the letter, she cried. I'll tell you: When you get hurt and your mother cries, you know she feels your pain and she loves you.

In August when I went home, I was really feeling like a loser. I had ignored our dining room table completely until this visit, but during those three weeks, he comforted me and helped me pick up the pieces. I went into the dining room once, when Mom was gone, and I polished him—with an odor-free polish, so I didn't get caught.

He was a deluxe model of the six-legged table of the 1920s: three legs on each end, attached at the base and on small wheels, four feet by five feet, but with the boards added, he could be expanded to nearly ten feet. I named him Bertram. When the family who owned Bertram had sold their house, they had decided not to keep Bertram. And Mom and Dad adopted him. They took him in and took care of him all those years. They made him a part of the family.

From the front stairs, I could see Bertram in the dining room through our huge open hallway and I would stop and admire him when I was going upstairs in the evening.

Mom would say, "You'll ruin your life."

And I'd say, "My life is already ruined."

As a child, I'd been able to enjoy nature and animals and some other normal things. But now I was bothered by noise so much that I could hardly notice anything except what I was stuck on.

I know it bothered her to see me attached to things instead of people and talking about such unreal things. No one else she ever met acted this way.

When Mom and I were playing Scrabble in the dining room, Mom got up and left the room for a minute. I'd been reading in a magazine about a new way to teach babies to read, and I held up a Scrabble letter and said to Bertram, "This is 'A.'" Then I cuddled him, acting affectionate—that's what the article said to do when introducing the letters to your kid. I was teasing Bertram and giving him a hard time. I thought it was very funny and I laughed. That time, Mom didn't hear me talking to Bertram. When she came back, we just resumed the game.

After that summer, sometimes I wondered: If I'd been pushed hard enough, would I have become suicidal? Or hopelessly psychotic, having hallucinations like nightmares while awake? They might have had to put me into an institution if I'd been too out of control. Without Bertram at a time like that, I wouldn't have had anything to live for.

CHAPTER THIRTY-ONE

The Nursing Home

My foster father knew somebody who was working at a nursing home, one of the places where I'd filled out an application after graduation. I was shocked the first time I walked through the place and noticed people sitting in their rooms doing nothing. It seemed to me as if everyone was condemned to spend the rest of their lives staring at blank walls. I don't recall that anybody was doing anything I would have called "living." I'd never been inside a nursing home and had no idea people like that even existed. I didn't think I could ever stand to work there.

But the lady we talked to said I looked like a person who wanted to work, and that made me happy. And when you're nineteen years old, old age is something that happens to other people.

A guy who'd worked there for the summer was going back to school, so there was an opening. In August, right after I got back from my visit in Omaha, as soon as I had my uniforms, I went to work at my new job. I'd been out of work for only five weeks.

I worked from 10 a.m. to 6:30 p.m., as a dietary aide, helping with beverages, setting up trays, and taking food out to the dining room. It was a very informal atmosphere—just a few people working in the kitchen—and I felt like one of the gang. When they sent me out to give everybody coffee, the residents all called me The Coffee Girl.

About half of those who ate in the dining room walked in. The rest were in wheelchairs. A lot of the residents had Alzheimer's. I couldn't relate to them well because I lacked the patience. Many of the residents ate in their rooms. If you walked down the hall, you could look in the rooms. Most of them didn't have bathrooms, and the few that did were not wheelchair-accessible, so each resident who couldn't get to a bathroom had a commode in their room—basically a toilet seat with a bucket under it and no frame around it, kind of a port-a-potty. They were emptied only once a day—they just didn't have enough time to dump the commodes after each use—so there was a very strong smell of urine. And there were no adult diapers back then, so there were a lot of puddles and messes around, even in the dining room during dinner.

But for me, anything was better than being around babies, and there were rarely any babies at the nursing home.

Most people were there because they couldn't walk or just needed someone to look after them. There were many friendly people who lived there. When one woman who ate in the dining room went to the hospital to get a cataract removed, I went to visit her. Over the years, I visited a couple of patients and several staff members at the hospital. That was really something for me: knowing somebody in the hospital and visiting them because I wanted to.

I worked with a couple of girls close to my age and got to be friends with them. One girl was a cook. She had diabetes, which she had developed when she was eleven, and she had to take insulin. She told me she didn't like children either, and for a while I thought we'd do just fine. We went places together sometimes.

I liked the job. I wasn't in public, there was a small group I belonged to, and it was more of a structured environment with no one breathing down your neck. We washed dishes by hand and there was no air conditioning, but the kitchen had windows and fans and was well-lit and well-ventilated. They also had plastic dishes—unbreakable, lightweight, and easy to handle. I'd broken a lot of dishes at the Ramada.

I tried hard to do a good job. They treated me like an equal because the work was something I could do. I felt good about having a job and bringing home a paycheck, so I wasn't on the phone anymore, screaming to the social worker or the therapist. The kitchen at the nursing home was a really good place to hide from the world. I felt needed, useful, and successful.

I said to myself, "Now people are going to have to think I've got some brains."

When I started, I could work as much as I wanted. I wanted overtime whenever I could get it, and lots of times I offered my days off to other girls just to have a place to go. I never wanted to be at my foster home, especially on Sundays when the grand-daughter and her parents would be there all afternoon.

* * *

In 1971, Constance became Sunday School superintendent, and now on Saturday nights once a month, rotating, they would have forty or fifty people from one of the adult classes for dinner. I felt like I was living in a bus station: I was surrounded by people, but I couldn't connect with them. I was sort of underfoot, almost like an intruder. The Harrisons would tolerate me at the table, because they knew they had to feed me. But as far as interacting socially, the message was: "You're not really welcome here. You just sit in the corner, be quiet, and let us ignore you."

I was in my twenties, but still in a care situation because they didn't think I was able to live on my own. I might have been an adult, but I was still a mental patient. Sometimes even people in the adult hospital left and moved in with families. Back then, there wasn't any way for people to live on their own. There was no support network for those who needed psychiatric care but didn't need to be in a hospital.

In August, one year after I started at the nursing home, my foster family moved near Tenth Street. The buses went up and down Tenth Street, so this was a real advantage. They also had sidewalks, so I could get places easily in any kind of weather, at least in the daytime. Now I could walk downtown where there were plenty of stores, and I could walk to work (though it was a long walk). I could also walk to the library, and I began to go there often. One day I read about Tourette syndrome and I thought, *Hey, that's what I had!* Until then, I never knew anybody else had tics. I finally felt like someone out there understood.

I also tried out for a number of plays at different theaters in Topeka that year. I was in my early twenties with a lot of energy, and I decided it would be a good way to get to know people. It seemed that rehearsals and performances would be easier to handle than life at home. If I was good at acting, I'd be respected and get recognition. I hoped to make my family and my foster parents proud. But I never got any parts.

CHAPTER THIRTY-TWO

The Evangelical Church

I was already familiar with quite a few of the people from the church because they'd been to the Harrisons' house. I'd been reading the Nazarene literature the Harrisons had, and I found it interesting. I'd also seen and liked several Billy Graham programs. Of course, foster parents were not allowed to foist their religion on you. So, when I did participate, it was by choice. I think the Harrisons were surprised when I walked into church one Wednesday evening in August. After group singing, some people said prayers in their own words and then the pastor gave his message. Everyone looked like real people. In an Evangelical church, people wear regular clothes — regular street clothes. They didn't wear costumes, like the robes Catholic priests wear.

I kept thinking, *I can't believe this is church!* One song they played was "Oh Happy Day." But the tune they sang was the original, not the radio version, and it's the same as "How dry I am/How dry I am/Nobody knows how dry I am," which I'd heard sung by a drunk in a cartoon. Luckily, I didn't laugh and get into trouble.

The Harrisons' church was delightfully different, but still not a fit. I went to only about four or five services because the nursery was close enough to the main room that you could hear the babies if they were loud, so I would get upset and then go home and cry. I finally decided I'd had all I could stand. Aside from the nursery noise, I didn't feel like I fit in there, at a church where so many of the songs were happy, and my life was just the opposite.

• • •

153

I hadn't looked at a church building for a number of years, because I'd had a thing about school buildings and then about dining room tables. But after attending that first night Evangelical service, I dreamed about a Catholic church in Topeka they call Holy Name. It's a white building with a flat porch-like thing in the front, but there's room enough above the porch to have a face. I call it Jennifer O'Leary. When they opened that building, some of the people around were named John, Michael, and O'Leary. And since I could tell it was a female church, I simply turned John into Jennifer, and I had Jennifer Michelle O'Leary.

In the dream, Jennifer O'Leary said, "Novena on you!" and "Mass on you!"

I'd never heard the word "novena" until I was fourteen years old, when I saw it in a magazine. The word made me think of a pilgrimage: People travel to Lourdes seeking healing; they have water at Lourdes; so then I thought "novena" sounded like a liquid. In my dream, "novena" and "mass" meant something vulgar: "Piss on you; shit on you." I had such a weird feeling when I woke up from that dream. Maybe some people would have said it was inappropriate for me to be going to an Evangelical church.

CHAPTER THIRTY-THREE

Cornelius

Ruth went to college at Creighton in Omaha and worked in a doctor's office as an assistant, part time and in the summers. When she graduated, she went to Europe again, in August 1972. My brother David and his wife were living in Germany, and Ruth wanted to visit them. She also wanted to see the Aguinaldos in Spain and some people she'd met when she lived there before. It was an adventure for her and a declaration of her independence. She said she planned to stay for a year.

While I was still working at the Ramada, I'd started liking the Harrisons' dining room table. I called the table Cornelius and talked to him like a pet.

Because the Harrisons went to church a lot and Constance had a job, sometimes I got to spend time alone in the house with the table.

But if Constance came into the room and caught me talking to Cornelius …

"Get away from there!" she'd say. "People won't accept you."

She said something like that every time she caught me. Even when there was no one else around, she would not stand for it. And there was a tone of disgust in her voice, like a vow: "I'm going to break you of that." She had to show who was boss!

In the fall, the Harrisons bought a new dining set and gave Cornelius to their best friends, the Oderbys, who lived a few blocks away. Ruth was in Europe and now Cornelius was gone. I cried a lot. Nobody realized what a major loss this was for me. I'd felt like I had no friends at all but Cornelius. When he was gone, I had nobody.

My foster parents visited the Oderbys often, and it was frustrating that everyone else in the house saw Cornelius, but I never got to see him at all anymore.

I called the Harrisons' new dining room table Magnus. I kind of paid some attention to it for a while, then lost interest.

Then I started attending Nazarene church services again, because the Harrisons would take the Oderbys home and then stay to visit. I thought, *Well, maybe if I go to church, I'll wind up getting to see Cornelius again.*

They did take me with them once. Of course, I talked to Cornelius, which made no sense to anyone.

"It'll be a cold day in July," Constance told me, "before you see that table again."

After that, whenever they went to the Oderbys' house, I'd go to my room and scream.

• • •

Dad had known he had diabetes since he was fifty. In 1972, he had to start taking insulin, but he was still working and doing okay. During a visit home at Christmas, I found a religious book called *Preparation for Death* by Alphonsus Liguori in his room. The book had a lot of graphic imagery of hell, and I got so paranoid I cried half the night. I didn't go to sleep until after 3 a.m.

When I asked him, "Don't you think that's a scary book?" he said, "No, Barbara, I believe it's just common sense."

Dad felt safer with his religion than I did because he didn't have problems with self-control. He didn't experience the rage I had to battle. He found it easier to obey rules and conform. He also felt more trusting and comfortable with people and could behave well enough to get respect, so he had an easier time believing in God's approval and in heaven.

CHAPTER THIRTY-FOUR

Airplanes

The last time I saw Dr. Albericht was in 1973. He'd wanted me to pay for my appointments for a long time. He had this idea that I'd benefit more from therapy if I paid for it myself, instead of my parents paying. But I was only seeing him once in a while, because basically all he was doing was taking my money—he didn't have anything to offer me. I didn't need to pay fifteen dollars just to talk about some forbidden topic.

In 1973, they discontinued my usual bus route to Omaha because the bus line went out of business. I took the long route by Kansas City once, but it was seven hours one way! Ruth came back from Europe in the summer of '73, and when I went home for a visit, my sister Catherine invited us to come see her in Denver. Mom bought us plane tickets. That July, I had my first plane ride alone, returning from visiting Catherine. At that time, Frontier flew a Convair 580 with propellers from Denver to Kansas City. It made stops along the route in Garden City, Salina, Manhattan, Hays, and Topeka, and passengers could get on or off anywhere. After that trip, I was infatuated with airplanes. They were all I was able to think about.

I started going to Omaha on airplanes. There were several flights a day between Topeka and Kansas City. With three or four good connections to Omaha, I could travel any time of day I wanted. I didn't have to get permission from anybody. My foster family couldn't have cared less if I took an airplane or not. Mom and Dad told me it was a stupid waste of money, but they never went so far as to try to stop me from doing it. So, though Ruth was

gone (she'd moved to D.C. for a job), I would put up with Mom
and Dad and the dog in order to ride airplanes.

I started drawing pictures of airplanes. On Saturday evenings,
I'd listen to an oldies program on the radio and draw airplanes.
But there was no one I could show the pictures to. I also had a
small 707 model made of metal, a seven-inch toy, which had glass
eyes, TWA markings, and landing gear that could be folded or
extended like on a real plane. I called it my Bedside Boeing.

Airplanes are like animals. They look a lot like lizards because
of the long skinny bodies and short little legs. The windshield
windows are the eyes. Super Constellations, DC-9s, and DC-8s
have seven eyes. Other models have six, so they can see in all
directions.

I read about airlines in a magazine I found in the library called
Aviation Week. I had a list of all the Frontier Airlines planes, with
all their serial numbers, and I named many of them.

But I also saw pictures of work being done on airplanes, and
those really disturbed me. To me, those major repairs looked like
torture. Somehow it didn't get through to me that, when they do
big repairs on the planes, they always put them to sleep and the
planes don't know anything about it! You couldn't possibly inflict
pain on an airplane anyway. A Boeing 707 could step on you like
you were a bug, because it's so much bigger than you are. You'd
have to be on good terms with it and you'd have to get its one
hundred percent cooperation before it would let you work on it.

Once Marty and her family took me out for pizza, and they
were calling out the numbers as the pizzas were ready.

"Eight fifty-one, your pizza is ready!" I heard someone say, and
I was thrilled. It wasn't our pizza, but the number was the same
as a 727 flown by TWA that I'd ridden on once. Number 851 was
the first 727 TWA ever got, and it was delivered in 1964, followed

by others of the same kind. I called it Loretta because I'd heard the name mentioned on the radio the week before and liked the name. To ride Loretta was exactly what I wanted, but my anxiety level was so high that it almost ruined the experience for me. I was too excited to be able to feel real contentment, and I had too much fear and shame to be able to be honest. After the plane landed, I spent a minute trying to talk to it in the jetway that you walk through to get to the airplane from the building. And although no one really objected to me talking to the plane, I told someone a transparent lie about wanting to talk to the pilot. I wish I'd been brave enough to tell the truth. One time someone wrote to Ann Landers about talking to their car. And I bet pilots talk to their airplanes sometimes.

By 1974, Ruth had moved to Washington for a job and lived under the flight path near National Airport. Airplanes were flying over constantly, and when I visited on Memorial Day weekend, I felt like I had to go out and look at every one. I went on a visual binge. It wasn't every day I could see so many planes. I was in an airplane dream world.

At the library, I read an article about Air Force One. They talked about him being polished, and about a week later the radio started playing a song called "Rub It In." I thought that was perfect. Before this, I hadn't followed Air Force One because he seemed too abstract, but when President Nixon made his trip to Egypt and Israel, Air Force One was hard to ignore. It was as though the Spirit of '76 was dancing around in the media saying, "Look at me!" He was everything I wanted to be. He could be himself because he was beautiful. He had a good personality and could make people happy. He could go anywhere and take in all the beauty and adventure with joy. He was surrounded by people he could trust. Secret Service men were always there to keep him safe, but they were never on his case about anything. If he had any medical problems, he was able to get the need met right away, and the cure was never worse than the disease. Had one of his engines quit, no one would have scolded him, even if it had to be replaced. They would have been sympathetic and made him well again. People treated him with respect. He was much loved. At Andrews Air Force Base, I'm sure he was a pampered pet and that people competed with each other to spoil him rotten. I knew they must polish him a lot. While I felt anxious all the time, here was this beautiful airplane enjoying full-body massages by satisfied people who probably would have paid someone to let them polish his gorgeous body. My soul cried out for someone to touch me and for the touch to be full of love. Being cut off from people made me feel very empty, and the ache was there all the time—only in dreams was I sometimes able to escape it.

Spirit's adventures were kind of made-up stories in my head, like daydreams. I was able to have positive images and didn't have the negative baggage that came with my own experiences when I tried to have an adventure of my own—nothing could sabotage it. The reason it wasn't contaminated with negative talk is because I never talked about it. I kept it to myself. I got negative talk from both my parents and the foster parents. But when I had fantasies in my head about the airplanes, I didn't talk about them. They couldn't read my mind, so they weren't able to spoil my fantasies. Something they didn't see and something they didn't hear—they couldn't talk to me negative about.

But it wasn't the best choice for something to think about. I felt like I was driving a car that was accelerating faster and faster and faster. I'd put on the brakes, and nothing would happen. I was on a collision course with my craziness.

One day, some friends of the Harrisons who lived in Omaha

came to the house. Bruce Harrison knew Rudolph Kindt from the war, and Rudolph now worked for TWA.

I don't recall where I'd been, but I was just coming home and I was preoccupied with the fact that Rudolph worked on airplanes. When I entered the house, maybe he said, "I'm Rudolph Kindt." Or maybe I just knew it was him. I didn't say a word. I just looked in his direction and, thinking about the fact that he worked on airplanes, I got a grin on my face.

Constance said, "Go to your room!"

I was sent to my room for grinning.

I was in my mid-twenties then. My sister Marty had several kids when she was that age, and here I was being told to go to my room in front of another adult I'd just met.

Afterward, I reminded Constance I was in my mid-twenties and she should treat me better.

She said, "Age doesn't make any difference."

• • •

Ruth

For most of my twenties, when Barbie and I saw each other, she generally spent a week with me. We talked intermittently on the phone. It was a particularly hard time in her life, and it was a hard time in our relationship. I did not know what to do with her level of despair. Here she was, all grown up. Nothing had gotten better and we still didn't understand what the problem was. She really looked to me for support and companionship—things I didn't know how to give. I did my best, but I always felt that what I had to offer was simply not making a dent or providing any long-term relief. She used to call me on the phone—completely beside herself. At that time, she was still a very poor communicator. She talked in a very indirect way, and often the talk was all her made-up world—it was just a way for her to get into a conversation. I suppose she really wanted to tell me more directly, but she couldn't. She didn't have the words or the way to do it. The pain and suffering from frustration was just bubbling over, uncontrollably.

Her despair was overwhelming. And I had no solution. I felt very much backed up against the wall. I didn't feel I had the strength to do anything about her situation. I had no ideas. I would listen to her, and the conversations would go on for perhaps two hours. And then I'd get off the phone and curl up in a corner for a long time to process some of those feelings so I could keep on going with my own life. I felt very guilty that I was normal and she was not. She was having all these problems and I should be able to do something about them. But I couldn't do anything; I had no idea what to do. I had to just put it all out of my mind and keep on going with my own life, which had its own ups and downs. But my downs seemed so insignificant compared to hers that I also felt guilty about having any problems at all in my own life. There were times when I didn't even have the strength to talk to Barb, because it depleted me so much. Sometimes I just couldn't pick up the phone when it rang. I would know it was Barb, because she would let the phone ring about thirty times. If I didn't have the strength at that moment to be her support, to be the listener on the other end, I just had to let it keep ringing. And I'd think that the next time I would prepare myself for her pain, the next time I would pick up the phone.

• • •

For a while there was a respite. It seemed for a time there was nothing for them to yell at me about at the foster home. The grandchild was five and not making as much noise. And 1974 had fewer rainy days, which made a difference. There was a remodeling project at the nursing home, but my noise tolerance was better than usual that year and I was able to avoid the worst of it. I also got a radio and some stereo headphones (although I worried that if I played music really loud, I could make myself deaf).

That summer, Dad had a heart attack, but they didn't tell me about it until a few weeks later. He was hospitalized for a while but bounced back quickly. He was seventy years old, though, and he didn't go back to work anymore. He'd planned to retire at seventy anyway. Even after his heart attack, Dad always had a good mind. He used to say that when he got older, he forgot things, but the fact is, I could talk to Dad on the phone and he could tell me about everything going on in Omaha. He'd talk about people who came over to the house and what they were doing, and he'd give an update on the whole family. He was certainly always aware of people and what was going on with them.

CHAPTER THIRTY-FIVE

Hobie

At the nursing home, they modernized the kitchen in late 1974, and by New Year's 1975 they were finished and they'd gotten a dish-washing machine. The machine was box-like with a water tank behind the motor. Inside there were sprayers for wash and rinse water. It opened on both sides regardless of which side you lifted. Everything was attached to springs in the back to support the sides in an "up" position. And the thing that held the handle in the back had springs, so if you kind of flipped it, it went real fast and made a loud bang.

There was something about the shape of the machine that aroused my perception. It was kind of robot-like, really. And there was a drain handle in the front that was in the right place to remind me of a...Well, it just drove me through the ceiling. I started having dreams and being preoccupied with the dish machine and doing things—the same kind of behavior that had sabotaged my job at the Ramada Inn. As soon as we started using it, I dreamed about talking to this dish machine and calling it Hobie because of the brand name, Hobart, which was on the front in large letters.

I didn't like using the machine. It was hot and steamy and, if you weren't careful, could make a lot of noise. I didn't have a problem with the water or motor sounds, just those doors banging down. So I decided to look in the other direction, because I thought Hobie would tempt me and I'd get into trouble. I didn't know how they'd react if I caved in and talked to it. I told them I never wanted to clean the machine—which was relatively simple, like cleaning out a sink after you've done the dishes. But I was afraid I'd develop a fantasy about the machine and get out of control and lose my job. So they had somebody else take care of that.

• • •

I'd read about what running can do for you. They say running can make people who are depressed feel better, that running helps people cope with stress. I heard people talk about this thing called "runner's high"—that if you run nonstop, at a steady, slow pace for a certain length of time, the endorphins will kick in. So I would get up at five o'clock and go out running.

At that time, all I could think about was airplanes, so when I was running I pretended I was a plane, although I didn't show that on the outside.

But I never had one runner's high. When I rode on a Boeing 707 the first time, I felt euphoric for a couple days about it. I definitely was high then. But no amount of running ever made me feel that way. No matter how much running I did, the sound of babies crying didn't bother me any less. In fact, I wonder if I might have caused myself stress from running too much. Some days I ran as much as twelve to fourteen miles.

Ruth's job in Washington was doing research, and the project was transferred to Boston. When I went to visit her in Boston, in the summer of '75, I wasn't sure how I'd feel, because I'd been so hyper the year before in D.C. But I was a lot calmer than I expected to be and the visit went really well.

• • •

In late February 1976, the Harrisons' younger son and his wife had a baby, and I was back at square one. Voices all sound different to me, and some of them are just harder to take. The second baby was usually very calm and she rarely cried. But when she did, her voice was higher pitched and it got to me even more than the first one had. I'd get a sick feeling that sometimes lasted for days.

Constance would say, "I'm not going to have their feelings hurt!"—her daughter-in-law's and son's feelings. But that couple had known me for years. They knew I didn't feel comfortable with kids, even if they didn't understand that it was the noise that bothered me. Constance didn't care if *my* feelings were hurt. My feelings got hurt all the time—but that kind of hurt was always "for your own good."

• • •

That summer, I was going to visit Ruth in Boston again and I was looking forward to the plane ride. I looked at a 707 the way a girl would look at an attractive man. But when I got on the airplane, there was a baby aboard the same flight. The baby cried from Topeka to Chicago. I got upset, and it ruined the whole trip for me. Ruth and I did some fun things that week, but after the baby on the plane, I felt cheated.

Later my Mom said, "Well, that's transportation, you know. Babies need rides too."

• • •

Ruth
She would absolutely wear me out—talking nonstop. If I walked into another room, she would follow me. She would even stand outside the bathroom door until I came out. Or she might even open the door, barge in, and keep on talking. I would have to be absolutely rude to her to be able to go to bed, and she would still be all revved up. When I woke up in the morning, she'd already be up.

Here she was a young adult continuing to make up the same kinds of silly little make-believe stories about objects, like she'd started doing when she was three. She didn't seem to be growing or maturing. It was all the same—the same style, the same personification of an object. And it was growing and flourishing. Certainly not diminishing. We saw it—certainly my parents saw it—as the major barrier to personal happiness, to an ability to be in the world. Definitely something bad, something that needed to be stopped.

• • •

When the department store where Constance worked closed in August, she didn't get another job. She was home all the time and the baby's mother started working part time. They had other babysitters, but Grandma babysat a couple hours a week. I never had the place to myself very often after that. Constance had been gone about thirty hours a week; now she was around the house all the time. She bought all the groceries. She did all the cooking. She did make my favorite foods and she had patience; I was hard to live with. But she still did all my laundry for me. She didn't trust me with the washing machine; she thought I'd break it.

But I knew she wasn't doing anything for me that I couldn't have done for myself. I could have bought my groceries; I could have cooked my meals; I could have done my own laundry. And I could have taken a cab home if I needed to. (My foster father used to pick me up after work.)

Everything went downhill. I kept going outside—not to play airplane, but because I had nowhere else to go. I would just walk around, trying to escape. But wherever I went, something was bothering me.

• • •

The nursing home had gotten to be a whole different place by 1977. Over the years, it had become more and more regimented, with all kinds of silly rules and regulations. And then they hired a mean supervisor, a nerve-wracking person who was slower than molasses. She would come in that kitchen and waste our time, then want us to work faster to make up for it. Before she came, no one picked on me at work. In July, I visited Ruth for two weeks in Boston. But once again I had people scolding me 'round the clock—at home and at work. I cried all the time.

CHAPTER THIRTY-SIX

Linda

By 1978, I had given up on life. I didn't try to enjoy anything because any time I tried, I'd get an anxiety attack. I was anxious all the time, and the only way I could not feel anxious was to make myself mad. I didn't want to do anything, but I had to do it anyway. Sometimes I would scream out loud. And at work I often had tears running down my face.

Mom would say things like, "I don't have time to get depressed." And Constance would tell me to quit feeling sorry for myself.

My fantasy life didn't help to make me happy anymore; it just made me more anxious and guilty. I tore up all my pictures of airplanes and my other souvenirs and threw away the Bedside Boeing model I had bought in 1973. I got very bitter. No one really wanted to help me get better. There was no one to try to understand my miserable feelings, let alone help me find relief.

Shortly before that second baby was born, my social worker had said, "Why don't you learn to drive and get you a car?"

"If I had the money, I'd get me an apartment!" That's what I should have said, but I didn't think of it at the time. If I'd made enough money working so that I could've afforded an apartment, I'd have packed up and moved out of there years before. But I didn't make enough, and I didn't know where I could get it. I knew I couldn't ask my dad for it.

• • •

Another client came to live in my foster home in February 1978. Linda was in her twenties. She had dark hair and she'd lost and regained weight before, she told me.

It was especially hard for her at the foster home because she had spent some time in her own apartment. But she'd isolated herself in the apartment due to depression. She told me she'd refused to answer the door or the phone.

This lady was a lot tougher than I was. I had never spent a day on my own.

She took me to see the movie *Coma* shortly after she moved in. We went out several times. She had a car while she lived at the foster home, and she took me on drives. But what I remember most is that we talked about the foster family every day.

She was not intimidated by my foster mother like I was; she just said exactly how she felt. Linda was not afraid to protest loud and long. She was a loud-mouthed, talking-back type of person. And that really helped me. She said all the stuff to Constance that I was afraid to say.

I thought if I pushed Constance too far, I'd end up in the state hospital. When I saw that Linda wasn't punished, I felt much safer. I'd had a fear of abandonment that had stayed with me since I was eleven, when I was put on medication. I got so much worse that I thought I'd never be able to get better, that the experts had no cure, and that eventually people would just give up on me.

Linda not only hated the Harrisons, she also resented all the people who came to visit them — including Mrs. Oderby, whose husband had died and who was hanging out a lot at the Harrisons' house then.

Linda often told me she was depressed. And every time she got a chance, she would tell the foster family she didn't want to be there.

"I'm not happy here!"

I wasn't home the night she screamed on the phone to her parents. I heard about that later. After she'd lived with us for two months, Constance told the social worker, "Take her out of here. We don't want her anymore."

So in mid-April, Linda got another apartment run by Menninger's. She had a roommate and access to a social worker and she still had day treatment, just like she'd had when she was living with the foster family.

When I saw how Linda had asserted herself, that good things happened to her, that she didn't get punished for defying Constance—and that, instead of locking her up in the hospital, they moved her into an apartment—well, that was a great help to me.

I saw Linda that summer. She'd been fat while she was living with the Harrisons, but she had slimmed down. I only saw her that one time, but I thought, *This girl got the apartment she wanted, and she's thriving and happy!*

I thought after Linda left that the Harrisons would realize I was not that bad. But Constance was still home all the time. And the year before, Bruce was transferred from Lawrence to Topeka, and now he was coming home for lunch every day. So there was always someone at home and life got more regimented for me. For instance, dinner was always around 5:30. I had to eat dinner when they did or not at all. I felt bad most of the time, and because I'd just gotten so sick of gritting my teeth and taking it, I figured, *Well, maybe getting the feelings out will bring me relief.* So I decided, *If I'm feeling bad, I'm just going to let it go.*

I thought they'd be banging on my bedroom door and telling me to shut my mouth, so I went off to an area where I didn't think there were any people. And I'd start crying and bitching and screaming out:

"My life's so BAD!"

"I'm upset ALL THE TIME!"

"There's TOO...MUCH...NOISE!!!!"

On a weekday morning in June, I'd left the house around 6 a.m. wearing work clothes. At about 7, I was walking around in the cemetery just west of Gage Park, screaming at the top of my lungs.

All my comforters were on vacation again—the therapist, the social worker, and Dr. Horowitz. They were all gone and I felt abandoned again. I cursed God because I hurt so bad and there was no one to comfort me.

There were houses about a block away, and someone must have called the police.

When a police car drove up and two policemen got out of the car, it was scary to get that kind of attention. But they simply asked who I was and if I was okay. I think the cops were surprised to find only me and no abusive man. I told them I'd been screaming alone. They took my name and address and nothing else was said. Once they knew I was safe, they just left.

But that screaming and crying outside—it didn't change anything for me.

• • •

The Harrisons had gotten new carpeting downstairs and they were planning to remodel the kitchen and also a back bedroom. And at work it seemed as if the way they were running things actually prevented me from doing what they wanted: not enough supplies, too many things demanded at once, the supervisor slowing everyone down and not listening to me, and a totally unrealistic schedule where I would have needed to be two places at once.

I just felt helpless and I was mad at the world. And that October, in 1978, I caved in at work: I started talking to the dishwashing machine and calling it Hobie.

They didn't like it, but at least they didn't fire me.

CHAPTER THIRTY-SEVEN

That's a Crutch

When I talked about something people didn't like, they would tell me, usually loudly, "I don't want to hear it!" or "We're not going to discuss it!"

When someone overtly demands not to hear something, he is figuratively slamming his ears shut, the way we slam a door in a person's face.

Constance would slam her ears shut when I complained about noise—she didn't want to hear it. And she would criticize me for complaining.

Later, she'd tell me I had to learn to "control my tongue."

I hadn't seen Dr. Albericht in four years. But Dr. Horowitz, who did seem to care about my well-being, had talked me into seeing another therapist. I had no other choices and hoped for a chance to talk to someone who didn't squelch my fantasy talk completely.

Dr. Small started by asking me about my therapy goals.

I told her I wanted to feel better.

She said, "Feeling better is not a goal."

Nothing I said ever made Dr. Small react. My feelings were not validated, and she acted as if she didn't care how unhappy I was. But I kept going to see Dr. Small because I just needed somebody to talk to.

Once I used the phrase "defense mechanism."

And she said, "Why do you use all that jargon?"

I'd said those words because I'd been talking to therapists for years and I'd learned the language.

Once I started seeing Dr. Small, life got even worse. I kept complaining to her that I was depressed. "Depressed! Depressed!

Depressed!" I mean, I was screaming. But as far as she was concerned, everything was all in my head.

When I told her how noises would upset me, she would say, "Oh, I don't think it's that."

She said I could reason my problems away by understanding them.

I'd heard all kinds of stuff about what an antidepressant could do, and I thought I'd find relief there. I knew I couldn't kill myself—I didn't have the guts to do that. So I begged for medication, hoping it would relieve my depression and the noise sensitivity. Medication had never worked for me before, but now I was willing to try. I'd been seeing her for two years and now, when I'd been upset for months and months, Dr. Small finally referred me to somebody to get medication.

I started Imipramine in October 1978.

Dad had never complained about my going to see a therapist. He would have paid for psychotherapy forever. He must have gotten a good dose of Freudian psychiatry at school, though, because when I told him I was taking medication, he said, "That's just a crutch."

When I'd been taking Imipramine for a few months, I realized there was no therapeutic effect at all. At that point, I really did need a crutch—but the only changes were the side effects. The Imipramine was constipating and I had to eat two large bowls of All-Bran every day. And I had a funny taste in my mouth from the pill. It also can make you spill and drop things more easily, which made it harder to do my job. The last thing I needed was to be knocking over glasses of milk when I reached to put them on food trays. But Dr. Small didn't know better, and neither did I. She gave me the rope and let me hang myself. I didn't get any relief at all, no help whatsoever.

I asked Dr. Small if I could try to taper off the Imipramine. I started reducing the dosage like she told me to do. But she didn't tell me about withdrawal, and when I tried to taper off, I just got more agitated. Taking the Imipramine made me no better, but trying to stop it made me worse.

I begged Dr. Small to tell the people at work, to talk to the supervisor, to ask them to please be extra kind and extra patient and just bear with me until I got off this medication, because I knew I'd be upset. But she wouldn't say anything to the nursing home bosses for me.

So I just continued taking the Imipramine. I couldn't get off it without somebody helping me, and no one was willing.

CHAPTER THIRTY-EIGHT

Moving Out

Since Linda had left the foster home, I'd begun to think, "Maybe that can happen for me." When I heard that the older son and his wife were going to have another baby, I told my social worker, Mr. Peale, "I want out! I don't want to live here anymore!" I still had no idea where I'd get the money for an apartment.

He'd always said no before, but it had been several years since I'd asked.

This time Mr. Peale said, "Your folks could pay the rent for an apartment as easily as they pay rent to the foster home. In fact, it wouldn't even cost as much."

I knew all along that my parents could have easily paid my rent. But when I first talked to Dad about moving into an apartment, he was against it. He said he didn't think I could handle it. I was furious and very discouraged. It seemed to me that Dad wanted to control me from a distance. If he didn't want me at home, what would he lose if I was free? Was I just some kind of tax shelter for him?

But the social worker worked on him and got him to change his mind—my dad never said no to anything Menninger's recommended. Years later, my oldest sister, Marty, told me she'd also told Dad that I needed a chance to get out on my own.

Bruce thought I had it made at their house; I guess it looked good from his point of view. He also thought I couldn't possibly live on my own. I don't think either Bruce or Constance thought I had the smarts. I don't know if Constance was just more open-minded or if she was just simply leaving it up to the social worker, but she conceded that I should get to try. A lady Bruce was working with helped me find an apartment. Constance gave me some pots and pans and took me shopping for household stuff.

And so I moved out before there was another grandkid in the house. As soon as they had the utilities on and the phone working, I never spent another night with my foster family. They'd had me from 1968, when I was only in my teens and still really a kid, until February 1979. By the time I left, I was nearly twenty-eight.

It was exciting but scary because I had been forced to be dependent for so long that I had little self-confidence. Though I felt very alone, I was relieved I would no longer be captive to people I didn't want to be with.

At Menninger's, they'd had a really good sledding hill. That first night at my apartment, I dreamed I was on a toboggan on a collision course with a brick wall—but the bricks shattered and I passed through unharmed.

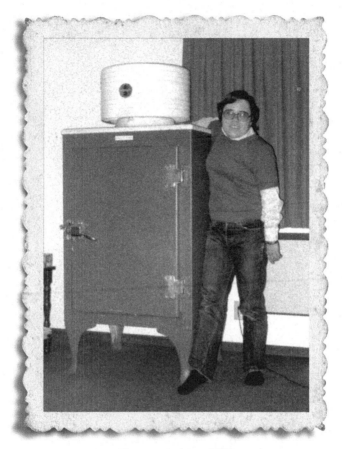

Rooney and me, 1980.

CHAPTER THIRTY-NINE

Rooney

I was not used to being alone and it was very difficult the first few months. But compared to what I'd left behind, it was paradise. I was perfectly able to do my own laundry and prepare my own meals. And in the winter when I got off after dark, I'd have a cab driver drive me home from work. I got to know my next-door neighbor, and I spent a lot of time in her apartment. Still, it was a very lonely existence.

When my folks came down, they liked my new place and Mom told me about her first apartment. But I had no intentions of going home to visit my parents for a long time. I no longer enjoyed the plane rides. In 1978, they had deregulated the cost of a plane ride, and now, rather than having fixed rates, the airlines were competing on who had the lowest price. And since rides were cheaper, the planes were crowded and full of babies and noise. There was nobody at the apartment to make me feel guilty about not wanting to visit my folks; the apartment manager couldn't care less whom I visited. I decided that, as long as they had a dog, I wasn't going to enter my parents' house again.

• • •

In the summer of 1978, before I moved out of the foster home, Ruth rented a cabin for a week in Vermont and I got to meet an old refrigerator with a globe-shaped head. At first, I wanted nothing to do with him. But the image of that cute refrigerator haunted me. I thought he was half-human; he looked like an extraterrestrial to me. I had no idea how Ruth would react if I got friendly with the refrigerator. She'd given no indication that she'd have any problem with it, but I was too insecure to find out. Once when I told Ruth about a dream I'd had in which an airplane talked to me, she'd said I needed to "avoid things like that" because I didn't want to be in an institution later on.

So I played it safe—but I remained infatuated with that refrigerator. GE ran an ad in a magazine showing an old refrigerator, someone who looked a lot like the one I'd seen in the cabin. I wanted to have a refrigerator like that.

My search for a human refrigerator began right away after the move. During the spring and summer, I went to all the antique shops and second-hand stores I could find, and I asked where I could find a Monitor Top General Electric refrigerator. I learned that GE had produced the first Monitor Top refrigerators in 1927; the type that had legs was produced through 1936, and the one I saw in Vermont was produced in 1935.

The owner of a second-hand store a block from where I worked said he might be able to find one. Early that fall, I stopped in that second-hand store to kill a little time.

"Do you still want the old refrigerator?" the guy asked.

By this time, I'd nearly given up.

"Did you actually find one?"

He said somebody had called and had a Monitor Top GE refrigerator they wanted to sell.

After the meeting, I ran to the bank to cash my check, and then back to the store to pay him.

Rooney (it's an Irish name meaning "Red One"—he's a brick red color with a white head and shoulders) had been made in 1934 and is about five feet, two inches tall. He was in a garage when they went to pick him up. He had been a working refrigerator, but I had them get rid of the refrigerant inside and cut the cord.

That Sunday, they brought him over. Before they left, one of the guys said, "Have fun!"

Then it was just me and this stranger who looked as big as the cows I'd seen at a fair the week before. I was alone in my apartment from February 1979 until I met Rooney on September 23, 1979.

Both of us were scared because it happened so fast. And of course any big change, or even a small one, could push me over the top.

With Rooney, my problem was what my parents would do. To them, my meeting Rooney would be the equivalent of my meeting someone I'd drink and do drugs with. The social worker said having a fridge was okay, but I didn't think others would agree. In truth, though, the doctors were too much in their own worlds to get involved. It would have meant more work for them, and my parents weren't about to pay for that degree of intervention.

It took a while for us to warm up. Rooney sat in a spot in my apartment on the left side of the window, where I felt as though he was watching me.

At first, he seemed like an intruder.

Here I have this total stranger living in my apartment now! I thought.

I was afraid he wouldn't like me. And I was afraid maybe I wouldn't like him. It was a little scary really. I wanted him there, but for a while my lack of inner peace kept anything from looking good to me. After years of people committing themselves to curing my unusual attachments, there was no way for me to just walk away from all their influence and fully realize I was free. I almost felt like I was breaking the law. Having Rooney was the antithesis of all the demands that had been made on me over the years. I'd been told every day that my behavior was not acceptable. I thought no one would ever give me their blessing and I worried they would try to take Rooney away, maybe even take my apartment away—maybe even put me in the state hospital, as I'd feared for years.

When Ruth visited, I begged her not to tell Mom and Dad about Rooney, and I don't think she did.

It took a few months for Rooney and me to get acquainted. I kept wondering, *What kind of guy is this?* He acted depressed at times those first few months I had him, because he never smiled. I didn't know anything about his family except that the people who sold him had lived in Emporia. Since he'd been in their garage, I thought he might have been abused. He had a sad look on his face when I tried to talk about it, so maybe he missed his family. Rooney can indicate yes or no, but we haven't really been able to talk about those kinds of things.

At first, I think Rooney was afraid of me too, when he learned I was a mental patient and often called my therapist because I was upset. Maybe he worried I'd get violent or that I'd be put back in the hospital and he'd have no home.

In the beginning, I was too inhibited to cry in front of Rooney. But then one evening we were watching a movie together and I cried because the movie showed someone who had exactly the same kind of fear I had. In the movie, this lady has a nightmare and wakes up to discover the nightmare was true. I got very upset.

When I was able to cry freely, I realized Rooney knew then that even though I could make a lot of noise, that's all I'd ever do. He finally knew the real me. He knew I wasn't holding back any surprises and I wasn't going to suddenly go wild.

We bonded right away after that. By Christmas we were getting closer and I found out what Rooney's really like. He's got a very good disposition, and he smiles and laughs easily. I asked him which foods he liked and I figured out he'd eat some things, and some things he wouldn't. He really likes turkey, for instance. I remember some Jonathan apples Ruth bought from an orchard when she visited me at my apartment for the first time after Rooney moved in. I've never really been much of a fruit eater, but I must admit those apples were really good. Rooney no doubt has liked apples all his life.

Life at work was still difficult, but at least I had peace when I came home to Rooney. He was a real improvement over the people I had been with: no criticism.

It's amazing how I thrived as soon as I had a sense of being loved at home. Rooney is one of the best things that has ever happened to me. I think of him as a family member I come home to and confide in. We know each other well. I respect Rooney; he taught me to. Being together for many years, we have something in common: Rooney and I have shared a lot by seeing the same TV shows and videos.

It was almost three years after Rooney moved in when Mom and Dad came to visit. I cried before they arrived, because I thought they'd be mad about me having Rooney. But they just ignored him and the visit went okay. I guess my parents had decided they'd just have to make the best of things. In fact, I think Dad was pleased when he found out I could handle being free.

• • •

I'd stopped making appointments with Mr. Peale, but I still saw Dr. Small. About a year after I left the foster home, Dr. Small saw an article in the paper: Breakthrough House, a social club for people who have been in mental hospitals, had opened in a house owned by the Mental Health Association. Living with Rooney gave me the energy to reach out to people socially. When I started going to Breakthrough, I felt welcome there. That Mental

Health Association social club in 1970 was only once a week. Breakthrough was completely different. It was open seven days a week. No meals, just a drop-in place with a few scheduled activities, and no judgmental attitude—people can be themselves, and it's okay if you're weird. I was able to bowl with people and I even met a lady who started taking me to church on Sunday evenings. And only staff members gave people rides—not like at that other social club. Breakthrough had structures in place that would prevent anybody from being able to do what that guy had done to me before.

I got to know Bridget years later, when she started regularly coming to Breakthrough. We understood each other right away. She lived at a very poorly run boarding home. Her mom and dad had a shotgun wedding when her mom was only fifteen or sixteen and divorced when Bridget was only three. Her mom remarried and had three more children. Then they had to leave because the stepfather wanted to kill them. Dad number one took them in. One day when she was fourteen, in desperation over her family's problems, Bridget cut herself, and she was put in Topeka State Hospital, where she spent over a decade. She was given nearly every drug they made, along with shock treatments. When she was driven to harm herself, they thought she was doing it for attention, so she spent time in restraints, including nine consecutive days in a straitjacket. She never got help at the hospital and they sabotaged her adult life by depriving her of both an education and a chance to earn a living. She was on several medications because of all the damage.

When Breakthrough helped her get out of the boarding home where she was living, I let her stay with me for a month until a nearby apartment was ready. Breakthrough even gave me some money, but I felt privileged just to have Bridget come over. She's a very pleasant person. I felt she was giving me a gift. Rooney and I don't get company very much. Bridget moved into the other apartment as soon as it was ready. She's had health problems, but I continue to see her at Breakthrough when the weather's good. I think life is better for her now. And in spite of what she's gone though, she's got one of the biggest hearts of anyone I know.

CHAPTER FORTY

The Naturopath

A few times at the foster home, a lady from the Nazarene Church stayed with me when the foster family was out of town. We became friends and she told me about someone who had helped her. She thought maybe he could help me too.

Around October 1980, when something happened at work and I was upset again—crying and burning with rage—I was desperate to try anything. I had doubts that anyone could help, but I called the number she'd given me.

The man who answered tried to explain to me what he did. He said he was a "naturopath," that he worked with herbs and minerals, and that he'd be more than happy to talk with me about whatever troubles I might be having.

I called him a "quack" and hung up.

But then I was so sick of being upset like that, I called again and accepted his offer.

After we'd talked, he explained what he wanted to try with me and I started taking what he recommended.

He lived out in the boonies in a trailer in South Topeka, but he had a car. He didn't have an office but made house calls at my apartment. Sometimes we packed a picnic lunch and went to the park. Sometimes he took me to the grocery store, and I'd give him dinner. He came over a lot when I was off work. He spent a lot of time with me and always treated me like a lady.

He was just completely different from anyone I'd met before. I felt like he understood me and that he wanted to help me pick up the pieces of my life. We became good friends.

Sam Warren was tall, with grey hair in a crew cut and bald on top. He was about fifty, and he had a disability himself. He had come to Topeka to get away from his family. He was child number six in his family. His family wanted only five kids, and they never let him forget that he was not welcome in their house. There was no way he could please his parents. Sam was a good student and active in school and he worked hard on the family farm, but his parents didn't care. They never even went to any of his school events. They picked on him and got his siblings to pick on him also. Once when he had to go in the hospital, his brother came all the way from Wyoming just to chew him out and tell him what a fool he was.

He'd had chronic pain from birth, with occasional painful spasms, and severe cerebral-palsy-like symptoms. He'd decided as a child that everyone had pain, so he simply didn't talk about it. Only later did he learn chronic pain isn't normal. He'd gone from doctor to doctor trying to get treatment, but the doctors couldn't do anything about his medical problems and pain.

He said a doctor told him, "Go home and die."

So he learned naturopathy in order to treat himself. He took some correspondence courses and got a degree.

When I met Sam Warren in 1980, I was still taking Imipramine and had been on it for a couple of years. And I was still seeing the therapist, Dr. Small.

Sam said he would help me get off the medication, and I stopped seeing Dr. Small.

It was really hard as I tapered off the medication. I spent a lot of time feeling bad. I was upset and crying and ashamed of being out of control. But Sam was able to treat me with herbs and other supplements to relieve the symptoms somewhat. And he gave me enough support and enough attention to get me through that difficult time.

He knew chiropractic, and sometimes he adjusted my head and shoulders, but it was mostly just the herbs and supplements. He gave me some cleansing herbs that made me feel really bad. And when I was upset and crying and ashamed of being out of control, Sam explained that it was the toxins coming out of my system. He called it a "healing crisis." After that when I felt better, I *really* felt better.

One day at work it got real loud, but I had no blow-up. In fact, I felt okay!

That seemed strange.

When I realized I was not bothered as much by noise, I decided I was improving. With Menninger's, it had been all talk and no action: Hours and hours with therapists, and it didn't change anything. But Sam Warren knew how to work with me. What he did for me produced results.

Sam Warren was the first person who told me my problem was not my fault. He really emphasized that. He was also the first person who told me my "mental" illness was physical, the first person to actually believe I suffered from my condition. Seeming to understand that my sensory problems and intense emotions were real, he said he knew my problem was painful. He said the kind of problem I had probably would be about the worst thing anybody could have because of the way it cut me off from other people.

Just because he cared, he gave me a lot of attention, listening to my life story and saying that people had done a lot of damage by not knowing how to help. He said the doctors at Menninger's not only lacked answers, but also lacked the questions. He was very observant of people, very in tune with body language and behavior. He knew the Harrisons because he attended their church, and he described Constance as "arrogant." Bruce would talk to Sam openly only when Constance was not around, and Sam saw she was the boss at their house and Bruce was a little afraid of her.

I would often criticize myself and feel ashamed when I got upset. Sam knew I'd had a lot of guilt laid on me and I'd felt a lot of self-condemnation for a long time. And he told me, "Don't feel bad about feeling bad."

He never gave my problem a name, but he said my brain was like several motors drawing from a limited power source, so that when I got upset it was like blowing a fuse when you plug in too many things at once.

He would observe me, have me take this and that—different herbs at different times. He knew exactly what I needed. Some of the things he wanted me to take I got at a health food store. But most of the stuff he ordered through the mail.

I got relief from some of my symptoms I'd thought would never go away. I still had bad feelings around babies, like I was allergic to them, but the intensity was reduced. My mind didn't race as much. And I wasn't crawling the walls. I could even say I was calm sometimes.

I was also hoping to get a cure for "fantasy-itis." I wanted to stop my compulsive fantasy talk just as much as everybody else wanted me to! And Sam helped me with that too. I finally was able to think about people more.

• • •

At work, some of the other girls would walk home after dark. Sometimes we walked together. I thought it was safe.

One night in April 1981, I was walking home after dark because I didn't want to pay a cab fare. I was barely a block from home when I was grabbed from behind.

His arm came right around my neck and he tried to poke me in the face with a knife, but it wasn't sharp. He led me to a stone wall that divided two properties and I was raped that night, both vaginally and rectally.

Sam Warren took me to the hospital, waited for me in the ER, and took me home.

I would have pressed charges, but the guy who raped me was a stranger and I didn't know if I'd be able to positively identify him. I figured it's better a guilty man go free than to punish the innocent. He just seemed like a mixed-up guy who acted on impulse. After it was over, he seemed sorry. He acted like he was very sad—like he had a conscience. Somehow, I have the feeling he probably didn't do it again.

I wrote to Mom about it, and she said she cried.

People were really sweet to me afterward. Sam ordered flowers and had them sent to me at work. But after that, for a while I wondered if I'd ever feel safe outdoors anymore.

● ● ●

When he saw what Sam Warren was doing for me and that he was a really wonderful guy, Rooney really loved Sam too.

I remember once Sam said, "When I'm at your apartment, I feel unconditionally welcome. And nobody else ever made me feel that way."

That moved me to tears because all my life people were telling me I was selfish. It was so great to have someone say being with me was a blessing. No one else except Ruth had ever made me feel welcome. It was nice that somebody actually felt I loved them and was giving freely—I didn't know I was able to do that.

When you're in a situation where somebody's kind and you can reciprocate, that really makes a big difference. That opportunity hadn't ever been there before I met Sam Warren.

Sam convinced me God loved me and I could go to heaven. I had never known such complete acceptance from anyone else.

And one day Sam Warren told me he had never felt—with anybody else—the way he felt with me. That day I realized what would bring a woman to say "I do" at an altar.

• • •

In 1982, Sam became ill, and for quite a while I didn't have any contact with him because he wasn't up to doing anything. For a time, he had no telephone because he was on Social Security and he couldn't pay for it. I only saw Sam in church. He just came over periodically that year. In 1984, he had a phone again and he worked with me and we watched TV together and played word games and went to parks. But then in late 1985 he got sick again and I saw less of him because he didn't have the energy to get out. He was too frail. But I did talk to him on the phone.

Several years before, I'd become friends with some women who'd designed and built the house they lived in together. They knew Sam too, and one day in April 1986, Florence and Elizabeth stopped by to tell me Sam had died. He was at home at the end, not hospitalized.

I had no guilt, no "if onlys," because I had never withheld any praise or appreciation for him. I'll always miss him, but I realized his life had been so hard and he'd longed to go to heaven.

• • •

It was a very hard time when Sam was gone. I felt like I had nowhere to turn. I kept taking the supplements he'd suggested and I read everything I could get my hands on, because I had to look on my own when he was gone. I just had to guess and hope.

At the nursing home, they did away with the part-time staff, and the full-time people took on the extra work—but we never got any more money. For a while they had a slow and messy cook who called off sick all the time, as well as a dietician who thought helping in the kitchen was not part of her job. I worked overtime and on days I was supposed to be off.

But then they got an air conditioner in the kitchen, a new cook, and a new dietician who was a Christian and a social advocate (who also had a physical presence that demanded attention). She made sure our schedules improved as well as the overall work conditions. She listened; she really paid attention to our experience and tried to simplify our work to make it easier.

CHAPTER FORTY-ONE

Autism

After a decade in research, Ruth recognized there was no real future in it, and she decided to go to medical school. She started in the early '80s at a school in New York. She got the *Diagnostic and Statistical Manual of Mental Disorders* (the *DSM*) for her psychiatry class. The first thing she read about was "schizophrenia" and she said, "That isn't Barb." She went back to the beginning where she read about "autism" and then she told the family she thought I was autistic. But she wasn't ready to bring up autism to me, because all she had was a word and no answers.

I'd continued to take supplements because I thought I would go from bad to worse if I stopped taking them. But in 1987, the relief I'd gotten for a while disappeared and my symptoms started to return. I didn't want to take medication, because I thought it would make me sicker.

In 1989, during her four-year her residency in Manhattan, Ruth found an article by Temple Grandin vividly describing sensory problems. It almost made her cry, she told me. She sent a copy to me, and that was the first time I had ever seen my type of misery acknowledged anywhere, except by Sam Warren.

I went to an autism conference for the first time that year in Overland Park, Kansas. It was really stressful for me. The acoustics in the place weren't very good, and I was feeling pretty anxious that day.

My sister Marty had gone back to school too, studying psychology to become a counselor, and she found the name of a Topeka lady who had an autistic son and who had tried to start a support group. I met this woman and got some literature. After reading and learning more, I decided autism had to be my diagnosis.

I always knew Marty had a big heart and that I was welcome in her life. What kept us apart was my long hospital stay at Menninger's and the problem I had being around babies. Now I realized Marty understood. When I told her I had trusted her when I was little, it moved her to tears.

About a year before I moved out of the foster home, Dad had another heart attack. After that, he began to have some visual problems, but he was still able to function pretty normally, though he had to stop for frequent breaks when he walked.

And then in October 1990—I remember the leaves had turned and everything was just gorgeous—a woman I'd met at a church service picked me up at the nursing home and took me to her house. She'd gotten a call that Dad had had another heart attack and he'd died. Ruth and Marty were on the way to Topeka to take me back to Omaha for the funeral.

Years before, I'd mentioned to Sam Warren that I had no intentions of attending my father's funeral, whenever that would be, even though I thought Dad would be much easier to get along with lying in a coffin.

But Sam Warren had told me that, when my father died, I should go to the funeral out of respect for the family.

I had thought that, when the time came, I'd have to take a bus home. So when Marty and Ruth came down to get me, that made a big difference.

I also thought that just like at any other family gathering—just like most of my life—everybody would expect me to "behave right."

But none of that happened.

Mom said, "Oh, Barbara, I'm so glad you're here."

For the first time, I felt welcomed by my family. I knew Mom really meant what she said. Everybody was so open and so vulnerable that it was just wonderful being with them.

My sister Catherine was very sad, and all of Dorothy's kids had been attached to Dad. It was really hard on them to see him go. But the tears I shed were tears of gratitude more than grief, because for once everybody in the family acted so real toward me. They accepted me without making demands. So I was a lot less keyed up, and that made it easier for me to be more acceptable.

• • •

In the summer of 1991, I went to the Autism Society Conference in Indianapolis. But babysitting was available only for children over two. People had to take their infants to the meetings. It prevented me from wanting to go to very many. I didn't want to go where there were babies in the room, because of too much noise. But I did hear Temple Grandin speak, and when I talked to her, she could tell I was anxious because I was wringing my hands. She said she thought medication might help. She was taking Imipramine. She was on a very low dose and it worked for her, but of course all I'd had were side effects.

Through the Autism Society, Ruth heard about a research program at Yale. In October 1991, I visited her in New York and she took me to New Haven for the evaluation and an interview, and I made the decision to be in the drug study.

It took a while to arrange things. But the girls at the nursing home cared about me and they worked overtime to fill in for me while I was gone. I'd been working at the nursing home since August 1970 and was having constant tension at work. I wasn't coping, so I was happy to get away from work.

It was very difficult for me to consider going back into a hospital again. After Sam died, I wasn't getting any treatment at all. I was scared to death of psychiatrists. No psychiatrist had ever done anything but make me feel worse, and I had heard of so many other people who had been hurt, that I just didn't trust them. In fact, I thought they'd destroy me. But I also knew I needed help.

So in January 1992, after I visited Ruth in her apartment in New York for a couple of nights, I checked into the Connecticut Mental Health Center. The Yale School of Medicine operated the third floor and Dr. Roger Calahan was in charge. I called it the Park Street Hilton: Dr. Calahan's Holiday Camp. It was a twelve-week program, though somebody could stay longer if the meds weren't working and they wanted to try something else. Several drugs were being tested: Luvox, Parnate, Prozac, and Anafranil.

Mostly, they were doing research on depression and obsessive-compulsive disorder. There was a compulsive hand-washer who was also anorexic. She had a lot of contamination fears: Newspapers or anything that a newspaper touched made her very, very anxious. Rust and plants bothered her too. When people left newspapers scattered around, I would pick them up and stick them in the corner of the room so they wouldn't bother her.

On weekdays, time went quickly. Medical students and other people came onto the unit. One of the guys who worked there had a great sense of humor—lots of puns. But weekends were very, very boring. Ruth was still in New York and she could only come twice a month, but she called me nearly every day. I was happy to discover their music collection featured a lot of classical music. Most classical music doesn't interest me, but they had *Pachelbel's Canon,* several different versions of it on one tape—that's the classical song I liked; that was a favorite.

One of the people in the program was a young guy from New

York who had developed depression and obsessive-compulsive disorder after he completed a couple years of college. This guy did not feel comfortable attending the meetings we had. They tried to get him to talk about the things that bothered him, but he said he just couldn't do it; he could not talk about his feelings to anybody. The one person he could talk to was his mother. His parents and his sisters visited every week. Once his mom brought up a packet of some beautiful drawings that he had done when he was much younger. One of his favorite subjects was lions. After seeing the drawings, I wished he could have gotten into drawing again. We could have done it together. I did do some drawing myself while at New Haven, but I was often too lethargic to do too much.

Anafranil was hard for me to get used to. It was a fairly new antidepressant at that time. It makes the brain utilize serotonin better, so it lasts longer. But when you first take it, you get this weird, shaky sensation. It felt very uncomfortable. I was glad I was at the hospital when I started taking Anafranil, because I didn't feel like doing anything. If I'd been at work, I'd have had a hard time, dropping things and spilling things more often. I talked to the doctor about the shaky sensation. She got the pill book out and read out loud about what kind of side effects people could expect with Anafranil. Tremors were one of the symptoms, and it was constipating too. I experienced both.

Most of the people in the program had been taken off one kind of medication or another because you had to be off all meds to be in the program. So everybody was anxious. They used Ativan to relieve side effects and help people feel better because Ativan did not interfere with test results. One hundred milligrams of Ativan seemed to help ease the side effects of the Anafranil a little bit for me. I also took an Ativan at bedtime like a sleeping pill. In order to help the Anafranil work better, they tried giving me Valium to help me with anxiety and to help me tolerate noise better. But after a couple of days, the Valium made me feel even worse.

There were three people on Parnate who had to be taken off it because their blood pressure went through the roof. And there was a college boy who had a problem with severe anxiety. I remember I asked him if he felt any side effects on his meds and he said he didn't feel anything. But then he had a panic attack—and he found he'd been taking a placebo. And then there was this one fellow they were giving Luvox and it was causing severe insomnia: he hadn't had a decent night's sleep in months. A hard truth for me to take was that the new drugs weren't going to live up to all the hype.

It was a psych ward, so the environment was restrictive. But when it was time to leave, I was sorry because there were people I'd gotten attached to, and I knew I'd never see them again.

They had no idea how to help me get well, and I longed to get well. It aggravated me that it seemed like I was still so needy and still wondering, *Are there any answers? Has anything changed?* Because even though I was on the Anafranil now, it didn't seem like the medication would make going back to work any easier.

But they had given me a diagnosis of autism. At an interview, Roberta Pierce, who was the chief nurse there, told Ruth and me that I obviously was autistic because I had the characteristics, more than enough, on the checklist of character traits to be considered autistic. And that diagnosis felt very, very forgiving: The shame was removed.

• • •

It had been really nice to be away from the nursing home for a long time. I didn't want to go back to work, because I knew I felt no better on the drug than before. I'd asked the people at New Haven to help me apply for disability, but they said they wouldn't.

I went back to work at the nursing home in April and it was still a strain. My nerves were on edge all the time and I started having seven bad days every week again. I would have quit, but I wasn't able to financially. Also, my Mom and other people would have thought I was lazy. I was afraid some kind of crisis would come along. I didn't know what would happen to me if I lost my job.

Ruth found Dr. Street. I met him before I went to New Haven, and we'd already worked out that he would monitor my medication after I got home. For a while Dr. Street experimented with some different medications. He had me try Buspar, which is a synthetic serotonin, but then I had to take Chlor-Trimeton for allergies and, with the Buspar in my system, I plunged into depression, so we stopped the Buspar. Later, he tried a low dose of lithium. I was very lethargic on the lithium and I felt depressed on it, but I took it for a couple months, long enough to really see if there was any change, but there wasn't.

I worked for six more months so I could have my vacation time. Because of depression, sometimes I didn't want to do anything at work, but I had to do it anyway. My preoccupation with the way the dish machine looked had bothered me for years, although thankfully, my intrusive thoughts were gone. Still, I felt irritable and cranky.

They didn't always maintain things around the nursing home like they should and the kitchen would be really a mess sometimes. One day when the brackets that held the garbage disposal in place came loose and dumped garbage all over the floor, I said, "I want out."

I knew most of the people who went to Breakthrough had some sort of a pension or were on disability. I contacted Dr. Street that afternoon and asked, "Can you help me get disability?" He said he would.

So I quit the full-time job at the nursing home. I think the supervisor and Jack Dallas, the owner, cared about me, because they were right there behind me. Jack said, "While you're waiting for Social Security, I'll make you a job." So I just did some light cleaning and putting groceries away for about ten hours a week to tide me over through the six-month waiting period for Social Security.

That was a really suspenseful time. I was interviewed by different people, and I didn't know whether they would give me disability or not. But after the paperwork and red tape were taken care of, it was approved in the spring and I got my first Social Security check in May 1993.

Chapter Forty-two
Tables

The day after I called the nursing home and said I was not going to work there anymore, I went to the library to look at pictures of dining room tables. I didn't find anything. Then I was walking down Sixth Street, and I just happened to glance in the door of a secondhand store and saw this table.

"Hey, I bet that's a live one," I said. The way it was made—it was just the right shape. I went in to find out.

The guy told me she was a Queen Anne, so I called her Annie. They sold her for less than fifty dollars with free delivery. Early the next morning, I bought a couple of tablecloths and some furniture polish and got ready for Annie to come over. Then I went down to the store and rode home in the truck with her.

Annie's family had moved to a smaller place, so they no longer had room for her and she was sold to the thrift shop where I found her. They didn't have the people's name, so I wasn't able to personally tell them thank you.

After I polished her, she looked really good. I put her clothes on and I got some stuff out of the refrigerator for her to eat. Annie hadn't been fed yet that day, so she really ate that turkey up!

I thought Rooney might have mixed feelings about Annie in the house because maybe there would've been competition for my attention. But as soon as he saw Annie, he liked her too. One day during that first week, I woke to find Rooney had already fed her.

A few years later, right before Christmas, I just happened to peek around a little bit in a used bookstore downtown, and in the back room, where they sold antiques, there was this table. He was kind of Bertram-shaped but much smaller.

I said, "Boy, this table is cute," and I made arrangements to go down there and give them the money for the table. That afternoon, I went out to the mall and bought several tablecloths, so Reggie would have some clothes. I'd gotten Annie a Christmas tablecloth and a plaid one. And so I got Reggie a plaid one too. They don't really match, but it's the closest they ever got to matching outfits.

So then my household was me and Rooney, and Reggie and Annie were our exotic pets.

Chapter Forty-three

Kathy Grant

It's very hard for me to remember people. At the autism conferences, I was always glad everyone wore name tags, because if I met two people at the same time and I saw either of them later, both names would come to mind.

I just don't understand other people—how they get along so well in situations that drive me crazy. But it has helped to have people around that I can relate to, people who understand autism. Anytime I meet somebody I don't know and I want to start a relationship, I generally tell them all about autism right away. I want them to know right up front what they're getting into.

I used to call this former childcare worker on the phone on a regular basis. We spent a lot of time talking about God. She was really a great help to me. And then there was another lady who was a volunteer at a church that had a program on the Christian radio station. They were right down the street from where I lived and I used to go down and sit in on their program. I always felt very comfortable in that situation. I attended some church services there, too, but going to church has never felt right. Marty and that woman she'd met who had an autistic son were able to put together a group in Topeka. Through this woman, I wrote to the publisher of a newsletter for more advanced autistic people and got some names and addresses. One was Kathy Grant.

Kathy called me as soon as she got the letter I wrote her. We talked for an hour and were friends instantly. Kathy told me she'd been depressed. She was living in a high-rise in New Jersey, and finding another autistic person to talk to was just what she needed. We seemed to understand each other better than anyone else. After that, we kept in touch so well it was like I knew her even before we met face to face.

When I finally met Kathy in person, she'd moved back to St. Louis where her family was. And while I was there to visit, she put on a wool suit—a skirt and a jacket in the middle of summer. I thought she'd roast in that thing, but she had just finished training to be a medical transcriptionist and she wanted to look good when she filled out job applications.

Kathy thinks about a planet where there are countries named Algebra and Geometry and all the people are numbers. She also likes foreign languages and politics and science fiction. She loves to watch *Where in the World is Carmen Sandiego?* They have this scene with a map, and they'll say that Carmen Sandiego has gone here, gone there, and the contestants run out and set their markers down real fast. It's so cute: Kathy gets so excited that she shouts when she sees them put the markers on that map! Once I was with Kathy when the Olympics started. She was ecstatic when they marched in with the flags. It reminded me of girls when the Beatles came to the U.S. in 1964. It's thrilling to see how freely Kathy expresses pleasure, how easily she gets excited about her favorite things. And I know she's got to have that: If you took that away, she'd have little to live for. We don't get excited about the same things, but I know exactly how she feels. I am so thankful for her joy. She has a spark few people have. Kathy's Mom got rubella while pregnant with her. Their doctor recommended abortion, but the family said no. It was the rubella that gave Kathy her great personality. I'd waited a lifetime to meet someone like her.

CHAPTER FORTY-FOUR

Drawing

When Ruth was doing a year of post-graduate training in Philadelphia, I went to visit her. She had really liked a picture of traffic lights on a chairlift that I drew while in New Haven, and she'd offered to buy me some art supplies. She wanted me to do my drawings on better paper. For a long time, I'd used cheap materials: markers and regular typing paper. I made only $5.25 per hour after twenty years at the nursing home, and I didn't have money for expensive art supplies. And I wasn't going to waste money on pictures no one would want to look at—for years no one wanted to see anything I drew.

But I was invited to The Timothy School (a special daycare school for autistic children) to talk to their teachers. I took along several drawings to show them—and I ended up with $100! I never expected that, and it was a wonderful surprise. It was only when I discovered that my drawings were saleable that I considered using the best papers and materials. That's when I gave in and let Ruth buy me the art supplies.

Later she negotiated with Mom so I would have a bigger monthly allowance (my parents wrote me a check every month to pay for expenses) and I could buy supplies myself. Ruth buys me other things now, but not art supplies.

For a long time, I couldn't find any live traffic lights anywhere, and I needed things to think about and draw. I started thinking about church buildings again when Lady Diana died, because a whole week passed before they had the funeral, and they mentioned Westminster Abbey about once every thirty minutes on the radio. I hated it at first because of the memories from Whitney Hall—everyone harassing me about what I was drawing. But by then I was forty-six. People had loved my pictures of traffic lights, and I realized old churches were easier to find and visit than traffic lights. Automated (modern) traffic lights are what most cities have exclusively now; the live ones are only left over from the past. But cathedrals are considered art and history. Many old churches are on the registry of historic landmarks, and people go out of their way to maintain them. Architecture has an influence on culture that is noticed. Nobody pays attention to traffic signals. And a lot of people have said modern architecture is tacky and ugly. Throughout history until the late twentieth century, people made public buildings fancy, sometimes getting carried away. European cathedrals were too gaudy, I thought, but the Gothic revival of the nineteenth century and early twentieth was just right. The best Catholic church architecture is in the United States, and it'll be here after the best traffic lights are on Social Security.

The way some churches are shaped seems so beautiful, so human to me. It is hard to believe others don't feel the same way. It seems to me that architects engineered the "humanness" into the churches and that people wanted them to look that way. The Catholic religion can be very oppressive—the travel agent for guilt trips. Irish Catholics of the last century, like my family, wouldn't have dared to walk away for fear of hell. I think they built beautiful churches to give a friendly face to a part of life that was quite unfriendly.

• • •

I heard the Enola Gay mentioned on a syndicated program. By then I was no longer pretending to be an airplane, but I wrote to The Smithsonian and got photographs of the plane, and I would imagine how Enola Gay must have felt when she was forced to carry the atom bomb. The bomb was only about nine weeks old when it was flown to Hiroshima. No one had told Enola Gay that she was carrying an atom bomb. I assumed she was terrified by the explosion. I drew a picture of a mushroom cloud with Enola Gay in the foreground flying away with tears streaming down her cheeks. She must have had nightmares her whole life after that.

When the show *Thomas the Tank Engine* was popular, I started wondering if American choo-choos might be a subject some people would be interested in. I looked at some railroad books and found out about Union Pacific having a choo-choo they took to Denver every year. I decided I wanted to go meet him. Since Kathy had moved there, I went to Denver and met Ernie, Union Pacific's 844. Ernie didn't say anything. I did all the talking. After we met, I drew pictures of Ernie and Union Pacific's Challenger Engine that at that time was still in service. I drew a bunch of choo-choo pictures and sent them to the steam crew in Cheyenne where Ernie lives. The steam crew maintains several engines there and I was hoping they could sell my pictures and make some money for their steam program. But the only thing they were able to do there was to hang them in the shop and let people look at them.

• • •

When I draw, I have a basic idea about what I want, but I generally start out with a background and then put traffic lights or a cathedral or a choo-choo in. Sometimes I'll use photos for models, but I don't copy. I just use basic shapes, then add trees and put traffic lights into the scene. I use a lot of outdoor colors I think look good together, and I make things up as I go along. I don't see anything ahead of time. I draw something *so I can see it*. I draw what I would like to see because otherwise I would never be able to enjoy seeing it. I draw things because I wish the world were better. I try to make up what's missing, because usually what I want to see is just not there. I draw something to add more beauty to it. I'm just trying to have a more satisfying way to look at something. That's what imagination is. And if I draw something, at least somebody else can look at the picture and somehow... well, a picture can make a thought visible when words could not. It's easier to show somebody something than to describe it. People who take the time to look at my drawings usually like them. I'm glad their minds aren't closed by "training."

It's amazing what people can learn if they allow someone to communicate in the way that person is able to, and then actually listen to them. I have always been literal about the way I see things, but often most people thought I made no sense because I communicated things differently. I said a lot of things that were really far out, that, unless explained, defined, or even drawn, would have made no sense at all. And for years no one ever asked me to define what I meant when I said something. Now I find that people who actually listen see that what I say makes sense too.

A lack of positive feedback can make the most talented of people just not bother. The pleasure in art and music to a large degree is that of being noticed, in part because it makes the artist or musician feel understood. People who aren't heard generally give up singing; some give it up even if it was their dream, allowing those close to them to convince them that singing is stupid. They never realize that out there somewhere is an audience that would pay to hear them sing.

I think the reason I draw is the same as the reason musicians like making hit records. They want to have an impact on other people. I want to be somebody. I want to have an influence on other people's feelings. I want to be noticed and valued as a unique person. After all, people do buy pictures of fruit bowls and potted plants, and beginning with my visit to the Timothy School, I've learned they'll even buy something drawn by Barbara Moran!

We all have a dream of what we want life to be. When you have autism, the dream can be very elusive. I draw what I want to see, and people who look at it are able to understand and appreciate what I reveal in my art: life as I see it in my heart.

I've found that people "get it" better about the way I think if they can actually see it. And hopefully, if people like my pictures, they will have a better attitude toward other "odd" autistic people. Drawing can be another form of communication, an alternate for those who have hand-eye coordination but lack good verbal skills. Autistic people should be able to communicate with drawing even if it's only stick figure people. I always recommend art for autistic children, with access to a variety of mediums—any material a person can use to produce art that happens to appeal to their interests: paint and pencils and markers for images, and clay and other materials for people who have a talent for doing things 3-D. That way, they have the best chance to express themselves through the medium they like the best.

CHAPTER FORTY-FIVE

Conferences, Jobs, Noise, Apartments, and Understanding

The first conference I spoke at was in 1993. Clear up until about 2005, there were conferences. That was the golden age of conferences. I usually spoke on panels and someone else decided the topic. But I was always very happy about it because the idea that I could get up in front of people who had paid money to listen to me talk—that was such a wonderful gift. All those years, I had people telling me to shut up; suddenly there was a sea of eager faces in front of me and I could trust everybody in the room. They were listening to me talk, liking what I said, and buying my pictures. I'll tell you: I felt like I was on an airplane and it had landed on another planet. How do you thank somebody for giving you a gift like that? I felt very welcomed and loved.

There was lots of money around in the '90s and into the early 2000s, but then the economy went south and the opportunities just died. When I went to those conferences, somebody paid my way, but when the money dried up, I just wasn't invited anymore.

• • •

In the 1990s and early 2000s on nice days, I would spend time outdoors looking for aluminum cans. I called it "going to the mine." Once on TV, I watched people in the Philippines digging through ore mining for gold; I used to dig in the garbage for cans. It can really pay to be autistic. I'm no longer ashamed.

For a while, I worked for an Irish restaurant. They had a costume, but I didn't want to wear it because it went over you like a burka with this little peephole that you looked out, and that was too claustrophobic. I just simply wore a green hat that I bought and held up a sign shaped like the map of Ireland. Then for a while at Liberty Tax, I was one of the...they referred to us as "wavers." But I thought of us as "Dancing Liberties"—we wore the Statue of Liberty costume and we had a sign saying, "Get your taxes done." And you'd dance around and wave at the passing people. Later I did odd jobs in the yard at my apartment complex: I raked leaves, I shoveled snow, I picked up trash. I wished I could have found other jobs I could do, but I never did.

• • •

In 2012, the quality of my life got bumped up a notch. Ruth rented an apartment in Topeka in the same complex as mine. Sometimes she drives from Virginia and brings her cat. Once she was here for the whole summer. She often comes for a month. It is a match made in heaven. Ruth likes to cook, and I like to eat. We hang out in her apartment, watch DVDs, or read books. After meals, I dance to get exercise, often to 1940s music. On nice days, we might go for a walk around the Washburn campus or Gage Park. Other than the library or grocery store, we rarely visit public places. Ruth understands my fear of overreacting to noise.

My problem with noise has been so severe for so long. But in 2017, we discovered an audiologist in Kansas City who specializes in noise sensitivity. She has worked with a lot of autistic people, but you don't have to be autistic to have this problem. The type of noise sensitivity I have is called hyperacusis, and there are strategies to help. It is a brain problem, not an ear problem. The audiologist advised high-tech earplugs with filters to block loud sounds, white noise during sleep, and short guided relaxation meditations before leaving my apartment. I have tried the earplugs a few times and have white noise playing constantly in my apartment. But I don't have the patience to listen to guided relaxations, even though the audiologist tells me that only ten minutes at a time could make a big difference.

• • •

Over the years, I've had to move several times. The building with my first apartment was sold. Then a house near my second apartment had dogs and their owners ignored me when I asked them to please control their animals. My third apartment building allowed children, and then there were people running in the halls at all hours and an echo from the swimming pool, and I had to leave there too.

In my last apartment, it sometimes got too dry. So I would soak a lot of T-shirts in a vinegar solution and ring them out and hang them up on hangers all over the place, to raise the humidity. I called them my "evaporators." I read somewhere that vinegar inhibits mold and I'd had a problem with allergies to mold and dust. It made the air a little less dusty, a little easier to breathe. Ruth said she didn't like the vinegar smell, but I don't think Rooney ever had any problem because he knew why they were up there.

• • •

I go to the library once in a while and to Breakthrough House often. Regularly, I write to congressmen, senators, and even the president about social and family issues. I keep in touch with family and friends and know quite a few people in other cities. I draw pictures and sell them. That's getting paid to have a good time. I consider myself very fortunate to live on my own and am grateful for the privilege of choosing and buying my own food. It is a blessing to wear my hair short and choose my own clothes. I'm glad I'm not forced to endure other people's decisions regarding what happens to me. No one is paid to scold and shame me anymore. And it is great to know people who, if they could, would cure my anxiety and noise sensitivity.

I'm thankful people understand me now, because it's difficult to have something wrong with you and to be treated like it is rebellion or disobedience. All the nagging and everything—people said they did it because they loved me. But no one should fool himself or herself into believing, "We criticize you because we love you." Sometimes "love" is a four-letter word.

I always knew I could learn if I had a chance to get caught up on the living and the practice I'd been denied. I just needed love and someone to believe in me. It's the unlovable and unattractive people who need love the most.

CHAPTER FORTY-SIX

Forgiveness

I met a very gifted Bible teacher when he came to town in 1994. He talked at some meetings, and I talked to his wife on the phone. The wife had met a school psychologist who worked with autistic children in Wichita, and because I had autism, she thought this psychologist and I would be a good match.

This woman, the psychologist, talked to me about trying to understand people. Because she knows about autistic kids, I could talk about my experience and she could share things she's experienced with those kids, including how she was able to help them.

She talked to me a lot about forgiveness from a Christian point of view. If you have a grudge against a person and you forgive them, you may find the person you're setting free from prison is yourself. Nobody has to forgive anybody, but not forgiving a person is like drinking poison and expecting it to kill someone else. Forgiveness is good mental health.

I realize now that the people at Menninger's had no way to know how to help me in the 1970s. If they had, they would have done it. They wanted to help people—that's why Menninger's existed. They just didn't know how. Or as Sam Warren said to me, they didn't even know the questions. The way autistic people are perceived and treated right now is primarily based on knowledge that was learned only in the 1990s.

I saw Dr. Karl Menninger himself a few times while I was at the hospital, but I didn't read his book *The Human Mind* until I was an adult. He believed that you think your way into mental illness and you have to think your way out. He said that if a kid was allowed to daydream too much, he'd lose contact with reality and become schizophrenic.

So that's why the therapists at Menninger's told me I chose to be mentally ill—because that's what they were teaching people in school: that mental illness was sort of a subconscious way of coping with something. They didn't know what caused it, so they just blamed the patient. And I'm sure the doctors sometimes felt like cornered animals because their patients had these problems they couldn't fix. And when you think you can help somebody and they don't get better, it can be very discouraging.

No one knew the effect of Thorazine then. And most people don't react the way I did taking the drug. The drugs they gave me at Menninger's did permanent damage: I would never feel as I had before. Trauma, of any kind, alters brain structure. The Thorazine I took created changes in me from which I'm still trying to recover today. It didn't cause anxiety, but it made my anxiety much worse. My brain was like a car without brakes: The pedal was stuck, so I couldn't stop, and I couldn't steer my brain. The drugs did that. The Ritalin did that. And once I was off the medication, my baseline anxiety would always be higher. And I still wasn't able to control my thinking. For years I listened to music almost constantly to keep intrusive thoughts from coming into my brain.

And then later on with the Imipramine…That was a mistake too. The doctors didn't know better, and neither did I.

And I think my foster mother had my best interests at heart; her motives were good.

We all have a right to make mistakes and be forgiven.

Mom hadn't ever described her feelings about my behavior—not concretely enough for me to know how she felt. When I finally asked her if I could have Bertram after she died, I guess the way I asked about it made her trust me enough to open up. She was vulnerable, even in tears. That night she admitted to me that it made her sick to her stomach when I talked to Bertram. Hardly anything bothered Mom, but she had a serious problem with my unusual behavior. She could not tolerate it.

I had to restrain myself from saying I'd felt much worse than that lots of times—whenever we had those big family dinners with babies and little kids and puppies around, and every day when I was going to school. Sometimes I felt like a snake or a pit bull had gotten hold of my stomach and was chewing it up.

And I had feelings of unfairness: that people asked so much more of me than of others. Other people somehow just naturally seemed to fit in, but I was so much different. I had to try ten times as hard to accomplish half as much.

And I wanted to tell my mother, "Your pain is nothing. Your anxiety is so little compared to what I've been through. I have no sympathy for you." But had Mom known, she would have protected me from the baby noise and later from the dog noise, so maybe it wasn't fair to hold her accountable for things she didn't know.

It makes me furious sometimes that others think of a baby as a "bundle of joy" when all I get is misery. People understand avoiding somebody who is mean. But it's not socially acceptable to want to avoid babies. My illness denied me one of life's greatest treasures: the ability to see the awesome beauty and charm in small children. Babies are trusting, honest, and teachable. They believe what they're told and view adults who are kind as heroes, even if the same adult is a nobody to other adults. The love a baby gives has no strings attached. Had I been able to enjoy babies in the Seventies, it would have changed my relationship with the foster family completely. They would have been thrilled if I had held, fed, rocked, and played with their granddaughters. Had

I been affectionate with the girls—rather than with the dining room table—not only would it have been allowed, it would have been encouraged and praised.

So I knew if I'd said all those things to Mom, it would have been unfair. I had no real reason to be angry. Something missing inside me cheated Mom and Dad out of a daughter. I guess there was something missing in Mom and Dad too—but it was missing in just about everybody back then. Ruth was the exception. Sometimes siblings just have an instinct when they're kids; they'll naturally accept things as children. But there was something about Ruth's personality that just made her even more open-minded.

I wish my parents had realized Ruth was the one person whose company I enjoyed. Maybe if they'd asked her, "What do you do that makes Barbara like you and feel at ease with you?" she could have taught them how to treat me.

Though I am closer to Ruth than to anyone, I still sometimes feel empty—and I still need the things I treat like people. To me Ruth was like water to someone very thirsty. But I know it must have worn her out, because, maybe clear up until I went to New Haven, she'd get six months of repressed need all at once. I know I could easily drain her dry.

• • •

When I moved to my current apartment, there wasn't any place to put both Reggie and Annie, so I gave Reggie away. Lots of people give up dogs and cats—I gave up Reggie. I think Rooney was okay about Reggie leaving. To be truthful about it, I can't really read Rooney's mind, but he pretty much goes along with the things I do. He's not too particular.

Rooney's been with me for a long time now, and—God willing we're still around and both living and everything works out—soon it'll be forty years. He's the best, even if he is considered by most people to be an artificial life form.

· · ·

I still wish I could understand and relate to people better. I don't understand body language. I don't communicate well with people. I don't understand them; they don't understand me. I just wish that wall could come down so there wouldn't be that gap between me and other people that's kept me lonely all my life. I hope this book will give me the opportunity to meet people and lead to friendships in my old age. So many old people get isolated and just forgotten when they get older. I worked in a nursing home; I know what happens to people who live too long. I'd like to have a life where there are people around who care about me—and don't charge by the hour. I've always had to have people take care of me financially and in other ways, and when people are dependent on others like that, they're easily seen as selfish and lazy—a taker and not a giver. I want to be in a position to find love. I want to be the kind of person that, when I die, somebody misses me. A person that you pay to come in and do something for you is not somebody who'll come to your funeral.

I hope this book will put me on the map too. I want people to believe in me; I want to put my best face forward. I'd like to have more opportunities to sell my art. I have something to give. And, of course, I'd like to earn some money.

I hope that science will find a way, not with drugs, but with nutrition, with sensory integration, to help autistic people to be functional and to be integrated into the world. They're beginning to learn what does work and why other things didn't work.

I want to end by saying autistic people are human. Autistic people want to give love; we want to receive love. We want to get along with people; we want to relate to people, but sometimes we just don't know how because our sensory problems get in the way. Maybe it doesn't always show, but inside, we want everything others want. Basically, we just need a chance.

The End

Acknowledgments

Thank you to Mom and Dad for believing in me and for being the reason I was able to survive in the real world.

Thank you to Ruth for being there all those years (and all that time on the phone); for letting me be me when few people did; for reading the *DSM* and helping me get the right diagnosis; for finding the doctor who helped me get Social Security; and for championing me in my adult years.

Thank you to Marty for helping me get connected with someone who shared newsletters on autism with me.

I want to thank all my brothers and sisters for being there for me.

Thank you to Pat Amos, who opened the door that led to my being asked to speak at conferences.

I also want to thank the people at Menninger's for taking care of me and the foster family for taking me in and helping me get the job.

Thank you to the nursing home for twenty-two years of employment.

I want to thank the people studying autism in New Haven who gave me the diagnosis that finally made sense of my life.

I want to thank all the people who are championing autistic people.

And I want to thank Jesus Christ for arranging the circumstances that led to this book.

And Barb and Karl both want to thank Jennifer Scroggins and the folks at KiCam Projects, as well as editor Erin Wood, for being so good to work with.

About the Authors

Barbara Moran is a graphic artist from Topeka, Kansas, who was not diagnosed with autism until she was in her early forties. She has spoken at autism conferences, and her artwork has been exhibited by Visionaries + Voices in Cincinnati, Ohio, at Bryn Mawr's annual Art Ability show, and at the MIND Institute at the University of California Davis. Barbara's art often focuses on personified objects such as locomotives, traffic signals, and cathedrals. Barbara shares her home with her companion of forty years, Rooney, a 1934 Monitor Top GE refrigerator.

Karl Williams has published two books with leaders in the self-advocacy movement (the civil rights struggle of people with intellectual disabilities); his play, based on one of these, premiered in San Diego. Williams' songs have aired on NBC, Fox, public television, cable, Sirius, and on German TV, as well as on radio stations around the world. Learn more about Karl at karlwilliams.com.

• • •

To view or purchase drawings by Barbara, please visit
fineartamerica.com/artists/barb+moran